# "HAPPINESS"

Published by Mindstir Media, LLC
45 Lafayette Rd | Suite 181| North Hampton, NH 03862 | USA
1.800.767.0531 | www.mindstirmedia.com

Printed in the United States of America
ISBN-13: 978-0-9985781-8-7
Library of Congress Control Number: 2017901289

# "HAPPINESS"

## *To be happy…*

*by* Ian Howard

MINDSTIR MEDIA

# FORWARD-INTRODUCTION

Rudyard Kipling -Words are, of course, the most powerful drug used by mankind.

"Happiness" is a collection of things we all should be happy for, and quotes from celebrities and lay people alike. Thousands of quotes to make you happy; to make you smile; to make you think; to appreciate life.

I often wonder why people take life for granted. When people almost lose the most precious gift one can have…their life, or they wake up to daily uncompromising pain, then a person might stop, look around and start appreciating all the wonderful things that make up our daily existence. It's time to stop and smell the roses. Before the roses are all gone.

I've overcome cancer twice plus other life threatening illnesses. The words found in this book, "Happiness" helped me to endure, survive and be happy.

To my Lovely Wife Melissa, and my two fabulous children, Brittany and Brandon…may we always share a Happy, Healthy life together. May you always have "Happiness."

# Chapter 1

## "HAPPINESS"

_____

No one gets out of this life alive...start living...NOW!

Ian Howard

**Things To Be Thankful For...**

The mess to clean after a party...
Because it means I have been surrounded by family and/or friends.

The clothes that are too tight...
Because it means I have plenty to eat.

My sunburn while working.
Because it means I am out in the sunshine.

A yard that needs upkeep, a house that needs cleaning...
Because it means I have a home.

All the complaining I hear about our government...
Because it means we have freedom of speech.

The ache in my legs after a long walk...
Because it means I have legs and can walk.

My big heating bill...  Because it means I am warm.

The person on the street who yells for a taxi... Because it means that I can hear.

The laundry and ironing I can't stand doing... Because it means I have clothes to wear.

_____

Tiredness and sore muscles at the end of the day... Because it means I'm able to work hard.

Waking in the morning... Because it means that I'm alive.

**Some other things to be thankful for....**

Love, Family, Friends, Vacations, Cars, Motorcycles, Toys, CD's, DVD's, Cell Phones, No pain, Computers, Internet, White Out, Jewelry, Clothes, Peace, Happiness, Togetherness, Hugs, Money, Watch's, Clocks, Mouse Pads, Calendars, Air Planes, Helicopters, Paper, Pens, Pencils, Rulers, Printers, Desks, Desk Organizers, Business Cards, My business, Job, Work, Endurance, Speed, Athleticism, Tranquility, Harmony, Touch, Massages, Stamps, Sister, Brother, Mother, Father, Uncle, Aunt, Niece, Nephew, Brother-in-law, Sister-in-law, Mother-in-law, Father-in-lat, Pets, Dogs, Cats, Turtles, Books, Magazines, T.V., Concerts, Plays, Notebooks, My mind, Doors, Roofs, Windows, Garages, Walls, Rain, Wind, Surf, Beach, Mountains, Sunshine, Clouds, Belly buttons, Toes, Feet, Legs, Backs, Shoulders, Necks, Heads, Sight, Taste, Tongues, Brain, Floors, Carpet, Tile, Furniture, Holidays, Jokes, Humor, Cold, Hot, Warm. **LIFE.** There are literally thousands of things to be happy for! I challenge you to write down 100 more things you should be happy for.

- I deserve to be happy and successful
- I have the power to change myself
- I can forgive and understand others and their motives
- I can make my own choices and decisions
- I am free to choose to live as I wish and to give priority to my desires
- I can choose happiness whenever I wish no matter what my circumstances
- I am flexible and open to change in every aspect of my life
- I act with confidence having a general plan and accept plans are open to alteration

- It is enough to have done my best
- I deserve to be loved

No good can give us pleasure if we do not share it with others.

**Seneca**

The chief danger in life is that you may take too many precautions.

**Alfred Adler**

Being right is one more good reason for not succeeding.

**Nicolas Davila**

It is not because things are difficult that we do not dare; it is because we do not dare that they are difficult.

**Seneca**

Whether you think you can or think you can't, you are right.

**Henry Ford**

We are what we think. All that we are arises with our thoughts. With our thoughts, we make the world.

**Buddha**

There is no stress in the world, only people thinking stressful thoughts.

**Dr. Wayne Dyer**

Nothing can stop the man with the right mental attitude from achieving his goal. Nothing on earth can help the man with the wrong attitude.

**Thomas Jefferson**

No one can make you feel inferior without your consent.

**Eleanor Roosevelt**

To preserve health is a moral and religious duty, for health is the basis of all social virtues. We can no longer be useful when not well.

**Samuel Johnson (1709-1784) English Author**

There is nothing either good or bad, but thinking makes it so.

**William Shakespeare**

Never let the fear of striking out get in your way.

**Babe Ruth**

Progress is the law of life: man is not Man as yet.

**Robert Browning**

You can have everything you want in life you want, if you will just help enough other people get what they want.

**Zig Ziglar**

Twenty years from now you will be more disappointed by the things you didn't do than by the ones you did. So throw off the bowlines, sail away from the safe harbor. Catch the trade winds in your sails. Explore. Dream.

**Mark Twain**

Positive thoughts keep you in harmony with the universe.

**Dr. Wayne Dyer**

Any fact facing us is not as important as our attitude toward it, for that determines our success or failure.

**Norman Vincent Peale**

There are two big forces at work, external and internal. We have very little control over external forces such as tornados, earthquakes, floods, disasters, illness and pain. What really matters is the internal force. How do I respond to those disasters? Over that I have complete control.

**Leo Buscaglia**

Our self image and our habits tend to go together. Change one and you will automatically change the other.

**Maxwell Maltz**

You are the sum total of all of your choices up to now.

**Dr. Wayne Dyer**

I am super good, but I will get better.

**Zig Ziglar**

Physical courage, which despises all danger, will make a man brave in one way; and moral courage, which despises all opinion, will make a man brave in another.

**Charles Caleb Colton**

To be able to practice five things everywhere under heaven constitutes perfect virtue... gravity, generosity of soul, sincerity, earnestness, and kindness.

**Confucius (551-479 BC), Chinese philosopher**

In the final analysis there is no solution to man's progress but the day's honest work, the day's honest decisions, the day's generous utterances and the day's good deed.

**Clare Booth Luce**

People are always blaming their circumstances for what they are. I don't believe in circumstances. The people who get on in this world are the people who get up and look for the circumstances they want, and, if they can't find them, make them.

**George Bernard Shaw, "Mrs. Warren's Profession," 1893**

True courage is not the brutal force of vulgar heroes, but the firm resolve of virtue and reason.

**Alfred North Whitehead**

Never speak of yourself to others; make them talk about themselves instead: therein lies the whole art of pleasing.

**J.E de Goncourt, "Idees et Sensations," 1866**

Hoping means seeing that the outcome you want is possible and then working for it.

**Bernie S. Siegel, M.D.**

There is no such things as no chance.

**Henry Ford**

Where there is life, there is hope.

**Marcus Tullius Cicero**

A room without a book, like a body without a soul.

**Marcus Tullius Cicero**

You gain strength, courage, and confidence by each experience in which you really stop to look fear in the face. You are able to say to yourself, "I have lived through this horror. I can take the next thing that comes along."

**Eleanor Roosevelt**

If I were asked to give what I consider the single most useful bit of advice for all humanity it would be this : Expect trouble as an inevitable part of life and when it comes, hold your head high, look it squarely in the eye and say, "I will be bigger than you. You cannot defeat me."

**Ann Landers**

Life is what happens when you are busy making other plans.

**John Lennon**

The joy in life is to be used for a purpose. I want to be used up when I die.

**George Bernard Shaw**

Joy is a net of love by which you can catch souls. A joyful heart is the inevitable result of a heart burning with love.

**Mother Teresa**

Live and work but do not forget to play, to have fun in life and really enjoy it.

**Eileen Caddy**

Those who bring sunshine into the lives of others, cannot keep it from themselves.

**Sir James M. Barrie**

Never let anyone steal your joy.

**Mike Richards**

It is only possible to live happily ever after on a day to day basis.

**Margaret Bonnano**

I think I began learning long ago that those who are happiest are those who do the most for others.

**Booker T. Washington**

A happy life must be to a great extent a quiet life, for it is only in an atmosphere of quiet that true joy can live.

**Bertrand Russell**

Real joy comes not from ease or riches or from the praise of men, but from doing something worthwhile.

**Pierre Coneille**

True happiness involves the full use of one's power and talents.

**John W. Gardner**

Joy is not in things, it is in us.

**Richard Wagner**

The art of being happy lies in the power of extracting happiness from common things.

**Henry Ward Beecher**

For every minute you are angry you lose sixty seconds of happiness.

**Ralph Waldo Emerson**

Such is human psychology that if we don't express our joy, we soon cease to feel it.

**Lin Yutang**

You can accomplish by kindness what you cannot by force.

**Publilius Syrus**

Constant kindness can accomplish much. As the sun makes ice melt, kindness causes misunderstanding, mistrust, and hostility to evaporate.

**Albert Schweitzer**

Kind words do not cost much. Yet they accomplish much.

**Blaise Pascal**

There is no beautifier of complexion, or form, or behavior, like the wish to scatter joy and not pain around us.

**Ralph Waldo Emerson**

Let no one ever come to you without leaving better and happier. Be the living expression of God's kindness: kindness in your face, kindness in your eyes, kindness in your smile.

**Mother Teresa**

A kind heart is a fountain of gladness, making everything in its vicinity freshen into smiles.

**Washington Irving**

Kindness is the golden chain by which society is bound together.

**Johann Wolfgang Von Goethe**

No act of kindness, no matter how small, is ever wasted.

**Aesop**

Man is a goal seeking animal. His life only has meaning if he is reaching out and striving for his goals.

**Aristotle**

You've got to get to the stage in life where going for it is more important than winning or losing.

**Arthur Ashe**

In life, the first thing you must do is decide what you really want. Weigh the costs and the results. Are the results worthy of the costs? Then make up your mind completely and go after your goal with all your might.

**Alfred A. Montapert**

There is no such thing in anyone's life as an unimportant day.

**Alexander Woollcott**

A great secret of success is to go through life as a man who never gets used up.

**Albert Schweitzer**

Oh while I live, to be the ruler of life, not a slave, to meet life as a powerful conqueror, and nothing exterior to me will ever take command of me.

**Walt Whitman**

Life affords no higher pleasure than that of surmounting difficulties, passing from one step of success to another, forming new wishes and seeing them gratified.

**Samuel Johnson**

Life is like a dogsled team. If you ain't the lead dog, the scenery never changes.

**Lewis Grizzard**

How do you go from where you are to where you want to be? I think you have to have an enthusiasm for life. You have to have a dream, a goal and you have to be willing to work for it.

**Jim Valvano**

Trust yourself. Create the kind of self that you will be happy to live with all your life. Make the most of yourself by fanning the tiny, inner sparks of possibility into flames of achievement.

**Foster C. McClellan**

The great awareness comes slowly, piece by piece. The path of spiritual growth is a path of lifelong learning. The experience of spiritual power is basically a joyful one.

**M. Scott Peck**

Too often we underestimate the power of a touch, a smile, a kind word, a listening ear, an honest compliment, or the smallest act of caring, all of which have the potential to turn a life around.

**Leo Buscaglia**

The greatest thing in life is to keep your mind young.

**Henry Ford**

View life as a continuous learning experience.

**Denis Waitley**

You can learn new things at any time in your life if you're willing to be a beginner. If you actually learn to like being a beginner, the whole world opens up to you.

**Barbara Sher**

When men and women are able to respect and accept their differences then love has a chance to blossom.

**John Gray**

Love and you shall be loved.

**Ralph Waldo Emerson**

Tolerance and celebration of individual differences is the fire that fuels lasting love.

**Tom Hannah**

Love does not consist in gazing at each other, but in looking together in the same direction.

**Antoine de Saint-Exupery**

Love is not blind - it sees more, not less. But because it sees more, it is willing to see less

**Rabbi Julius Gordon**

Love looks not with the eyes but with the mind; and therefore is winged Cupid painted blind.

**William Shakespeare**

We are all born for love. It is the principle of existence, and its only end.
**Benjamin Disraeli**

Think lovingly, speak lovingly, act lovingly, and every need shall be supplied.

**James Allen**

We are shaped and fashioned by what we love.

**Johann Wolfgang von Goethe**

Love gives itself; it is not bought.

**Henry Wadsworth Longfellow**

The love we give away is the only love we keep.

**Elbert Hubbard**

Treasure the love you receive above all. It will survive long after your gold and good health have vanished.

**Og Mandingo**

Love is a canvas furnished by nature and embroidered by imagination.

**Voltaire**

What we have once enjoyed we can never lose. All that we love deeply becomes a part of us.

**Helen Keller**

Love cures people - both the ones who give it and the ones who receive it.

**Dr. Karl Menninger**

You will find, as you look back upon your life, that the moments when you really lived are the moments when you have done things in the spirit of love.

**Henry Drummond**

Of all earthly music, that which reaches farthest into heaven is the beating of a truly loving heart.

**Henry Ward Beecher**

By the accident of fortune a man may rule the world for a time, but by virtue of love and kindness he may rule the world forever.

**Lao-Tze**

Love is not getting, but giving.

**Henry Van Dyke**

If you love somebody, let them go, for if they return, they were always yours. And if they don't, they never were.

**Kahlil Gibran**

Love is something eternal; the aspect may change, but not the essence.

**Vincent Van Gogh**

One word frees us of all the weight and pain of life; That word is love.

**Sophocles**

To fear love is to fear life, and those who fear life are already three parts dead.

**Bertrand Russell**

Grief and tragedy and hatred are only for a time. Goodness, remembrance and love have no end.

**George Bush**

If you would be loved, love, and be loveable.

**Benjamin Franklin**

Love is the beauty of the soul.

**St. Augustine**

The best proof of love is trust.

**Joyce Brothers**

At the touch of love, everyone becomes a poet.

**Plato**

Relish love in our old age! Aged love is like aged wine; it becomes more satisfying, more refreshing, more valuable, more appreciated and more intoxicating!

**Leo Buscaglia**

Just don't give up trying to do what you really want to do. Where there is love and inspiration, I don't think you can go wrong.

**Ella Fitzgerald**

Whatever is flexible and living will tend to grow; whatever is rigid and blocked will wither and die.

**Lao Tzu**

The greatest happiness of life is the conviction that we are loved-loved for ourselves, or rather, loved in spite of ourselves.

**Victor Hugo**

Shallow men believe in luck. Strong men believe in cause and effect.

**Ralph Waldo Emerson**

The only thing that overcomes hard luck is hard work.

**Harry Golden**

All of us have bad luck and good luck. The man who persists through the bad luck - who keeps right on going - is the man who is there when the good luck comes - and is ready to receive it.

**Robert Collier**

When I work fourteen hours a day, seven days a week, I get lucky.

**Dr. Armand Hammer**

Luck is a dividend of sweat. The more you sweat, the luckier you get.

**Ray Kroc**

I've found that luck is quite predictable. If you want more luck, take more chances. Be more active. Show up more often.

**Brian Tracy**

When I thought I couldn't go on, I forced myself to keep going. My success is based on persistence, not luck.

**Norman Lear**

It's hard to detect good luck - it looks so much like something you've earned.

**Frank A. Clark**

Depend on the rabbit's foot if you will, but remember it didn't work for the rabbit.

**R.E. Shay**

The golden opportunity you are seeking is in yourself. It is not in your environment; it is not in luck or chance, or the help of others; it is in yourself alone.

**Orison Swett Marsden**

Fortune brings in some boats that are not steered.

**William Shakespeare**

It's not what you've got, it's what you use that makes a difference.

**Zig Ziglar**

I will act as if what I do makes a difference.

**William James**

There is little difference in people, but that little difference makes a big difference. That little difference is attitude. The big difference is whether it is positive or negative.

**W. Clement Stone**

It's easy to make a buck. It's a lot tougher to make a difference.

**Tom Brokaw**

Two roads diverge in a wood, and I took the one less traveled by, and that has made all the difference.

**Robert Frost**

Often the difference between a successful person and a failure is not one has better abilities or ideas, but the courage that one has to bet on one's ideas, to take a calculated risk - and to act.

**Maxwell Maltz**

We must not, in trying to think about how we can make a big difference, ignore the small daily differences we can make which, over time, add up to big differences that we often cannot foresee.

**Marian Wright Edelman**

There are only about a half dozen things that make 80% of the difference in any area of our lives.

**Jim Rohn**

It's not the will to win, but the will to prepare to win that makes the difference.

**Paul "Bear" Bryant**

It's your unlimited power to care and to love that can make the biggest difference in the quality of your life.

**Anthony Robbins**

We all have ability. The difference is how we use it.

**Stevie Wonder**

It is our attitude at the beginning of a difficult undertaking  which more than anything else, will determine its outcome.

**William James**

When one door of happiness closes, another opens;  but often we look so long at the closed door that we do not see the one which has opened for us.

**Helen Keller**

There ain't much fun in medicine, but  there's a heck of a lot of medicine in fun.

**Josh Billings**

The greatest discovery of any generation is that human beings can alter their lives by altering the attitudes of their minds.

**Albert Schweitzer**

In order to laugh, you must be able to play with your pain.

**Annette Goodheart**

Nothing is quite as funny as the unintended humor of reality.

**Steve Allen**

He who laughs, lasts.

**Mary Pettibone Poole**

Pray to God, but row for shore.

**Russian proverb**

Faith is to believe what we do not see; the reward of this faith is to see what we believe.

**Saint Augustine**

---

Why is it when we talk to God we are said to be praying, and when God talks to us we are said to be schizophrenic?

**Lilly Tomlin**

He who joyfully marches to music in rank and file has already earned my contempt. He has been given a large brain by mistake, since for him the spinal cord would fully suffice.

**Albert Einstein**

Great spirits have always encountered violent opposition from mediocre minds.

**Albert Einstein**

Many of the things you can count, don't count. Many of the things you can't count, really count.

**Albert Einstein**

The world is a dangerous place, not because of those who do evil, but because of those who look on and do nothing.

**Albert Einstein**

I am enough of an artist to draw freely upon my imagination. Imagination is more important than knowledge. Knowledge is limited. Imagination encircles the world.

**Albert Einstein**

It is usually the imagination that is wounded first, rather than the heart; it being much more sensitive.

**Henry David Thoreau**

I know of no more encouraging fact than the unquestionable ability of man to elevate his life by conscious endeavor.

**Henry David Thoreau**

The world is but a canvas to our imagination.

**Henry David Thoreau**

That man is richest whose pleasures are cheapest.

**Henry David Thoreau**

The harder the conflict, the more glorious the triumph. What we obtain too cheap, we esteem too lightly; it is dearness only that gives everything its value. I love the man that can smile in trouble, that can gather strength from distress and grow brave by reflection. Tis the business of little minds to shrink; but he whose heart is firm, and whose conscience approves his conduct, will pursue his principles unto death.

**Thomas Paine**

How many a man has thrown up his hands at a time when a little more effort, a little more patience would have achieved success?

**Elbert Hubbard**

I do not think that there is any other quality so essential to success of any kind as the quality of perseverance. It overcomes almost everything, even nature.

**John D. Rockefeller**

The most essential factor is persistence - the determination never to allow your energy or enthusiasm to be dampened by the discouragement that must inevitably come.

**James Whitcomb Riley**

Your biggest break can come from never quitting. Being at the right place at the right time can only happen when you keep moving toward the next opportunity.

**Arthur Pine**

I am a slow walker, but I never walk backwards.

**Abraham Lincoln**

---

Champions keep playing until they get it right.

**Billie Jean King**

You've got to say, I think that if I keep working at this and want it badly enough I can have it. It's called perseverance.

**Lee Iacocca**

Our greatest weakness lies in giving up. The most certain way to succeed is always to try just one more time.

**Thomas Edison**

History has demonstrated that the most notable winners usually encountered heartbreaking obstacles before they triumphed. They won because they refused to become discouraged by their defeats.

**B. C. Forbes**

If I had to select one quality, one personal characteristic that I regard as being most highly correlated with success, whatever the field, I would pick the trait of persistence. Determination. The will to endure to the end, to get knocked down seventy times and get up off the floor saying, Here comes number seventy-one!

**Richard M. DeVos**

Perseverance gives power to weakness, and opens to poverty the world's wealth. It spreads fertility over the barren landscape, and buds the choicest flowers and fruits spring up and flourish in the desert abode of thorns and briars.

**Samuel G. Goodrich**

Some men give up their designs when they have almost reached the goal; While others, on the contrary, obtain a victory by exerting, at the last moment, more vigorous efforts than ever before.

**Herodotus**

Nearly every man who develops an idea works at it up to the point where it looks impossible, and then gets discouraged. That's not the place to become discouraged.

**Thomas A. Edison**

To persevere, trusting in what hopes he has, is courage in a man.

**Euripides**

Persist and persevere, and you will find most things that are attainable, possible.

**Lord Chesterfield**

Boys, there ain't no free lunches in this country. And don't go spending your whole life commiserating that you got the raw deals. You've got to say, I think that if I keep working at this and want it bad enough I can have it. It's called perseverance.

**Lee Iacocca**

Perseverance is more prevailing than violence; and many things which cannot be overcome when they are together yield themselves up when taken little by little.

**Plutarch**

Plodding wins the race.

**Aesop**

Persevere and get it done.

**George Allen**

Perseverance is not a long race; it is many short races one after another.

**Walter Elliott**

Sure I am of this, that you have only to endure to conquer.

**Winston Churchill**

---

Permanence, perseverance and persistence in spite of all obstacles, discouragements, and impossibilities: It is this, that in all things distinguishes the strong soul from the weak.

**Thomas Carlyle**

We make way for the man who boldly pushes past us.

**Christian Nevell Bovee**

The drops of rain make a hole in the stone, not by violence, but by oft falling.

**Lucretius**

Patience and perseverance have a magical effect before which difficulties disappear and obstacles vanish.

**John Quincy Adams**

All of us have bad luck and good luck. The man who persists through the bad luck - who keeps right on going - is the man who is there when the good luck comes - and is ready to receive it.

**Robert Collier**

It's easier to go down a hill than up it but the view is much better at the top.

**Arnold Bennet**

I had to pick myself up and get on with it, do it all over again, only even better this time.

**Sam Walton**

It doesn't matter if you try and try and try again, and fail. It does matter if you try and fail, and fail to try again.

**Charles Kettering**

Great things are not done by impulse, but by a series of small things brought together.

**Vincent Van Gogh**

Fight one more round. When your arms are so tired that you can hardly lift your hands to come on guard, fight one more round. When your nose is bleeding and your eyes are black and you are so tired that you wish your opponent would crack you one on the jaw and put you to sleep, fight one more round – remembering that the man who always fights one more round is never whipped.

**James Corbett**

Believe that man will not merely endure; he will prevail.

**William Faulkner**

We are what we repeatedly do. Excellence then, is not an act, but a habit.

**Aristotle**

The difference between perseverance and obstinacy is that one often comes from a strong will, and the other from a strong won't.

**Henry Ward Beecher**

Get a good idea and stay with it. Dog it, and work at it until it's done right.

**Walt Disney**

A hero is one who knows how to hang on one minute longer.

**Norwegian proverb**

The successful man will profit from his mistakes and try again in a different way.

**Dale Carnegie**

No man is ever whipped until he quits - in his own mind.

**Napoleon Hill**

---

Nothing can resist a will which will stake even existence upon its fulfillment.

**Benjamin Disraeli**

The gem cannot be polished without friction, nor man perfected without trials

**Chinese proverb**

Never discourage anyone... who continually makes progress, no matter how slow.

**Plato**

Decide carefully, exactly what you want in life, then work like mad to make sure you get it!

**Hector Crawford**

All great masters are chiefly distinguished by the power of adding a second, a third, and perhaps a fourth step in a continuous line. Many a man has taken the first step. With every additional step you enhance immensely the value of your first.

**Ralph Waldo Emerson**

Defeat never comes to any man until he admits it.

**Josephus Daniels**

The journey is the reward.

**Chinese proverb**

A man can only do what he can do. But if he does that each day he can sleep at night and do it again the next day.

**Albert Schweitzer**

Seven days without laughter make one weak.

**Joel Goodman**

Our greatest happiness in life does not depend on the condition of life in which chance has placed us, but is always the result of good conscience, good health, occupation, and freedom in all just pursuits.

**Thomas Jefferson (1743-1826) 3rd President of the U.S.**

We began by imagining that we are giving to them; we end by realizing that they have enriched us.

**Pope John Paul II**

In order to be a realist you must believe in miracles.

**David Ben-Gurion**

The most important medicine is tender love and care.

**Mother Teresa**

It is a curious thing in human experience but to live through a period of stress and sorrow with another person creates a bond which nothing seems able to break.

**Eleanor Roosevelt**

Life is a succession of lessons which we must lived to be understood.

**Ralph Waldo Emerson**

One secures the gold of the spirit when he finds himself.

**Claude M. Bristol**

Diseases can be our spiritual flat tires - discrepancies in our lives that seem to be disasters at the time, but end by redirecting our lives in a meaningful way.

**Bernie S. Siegel, M.D.**

There is in the worst of fortunes the best changes for a happy change.

**Euripides**

---

Happiness isn't about what happens to us - it's about how we perceive what happens to us. It's the knack of finding a positive for every negative, and viewing a setback as a challenge. If we can just stop wishing for what we don't have, and start enjoying what we do have, our lives can be richer; more fulfilled - and happier. The time to be happy is now.

**Lynn Peters**


What lies behind us and what lies before us are small matter compared to what lies within us.

**Ralph Waldo Emerson**


You gain strength, courage, and confidence by every experience in which you really stop to look fear in the face. You are able to say to yourself, "I lived through this horror. I can take the next thing that comes along.

**Eleanor Roosevelt, "You Learn by Living," 1960**


Your life, your achievement, your happiness, your person are of paramount importance. Live up to your highest vision of yourself no matter what the circumstances you might encounter.

**Ayn Rand, novelist/philosopher,**
**from "Ayn Rand: a sense of life" by Michael Paxton**


Liberal education develops a sense of right, duty and honor; and more and more in the modern world, large business rests on rectitude and honor as well as good judgment.

**Charles W. Eliot**


Nature does not bestow virtue; to be good is an art.

**Seneca**

I run great risk of failing. It may be that I shall encounter ruin where I look for reputation and a career of honor. The chances are perhaps more in favor of ruin than of success. But, whatever may be the chances, I shall go on as long as any means of carrying on the fight are at my disposal.

**Anthony Trollope, from his novel "Can You Forgive Her?"**

The most important thing a father can do for his children is to love their mother.

**Theodore Hesburgh, Readers Digest, January 1963**

You cannot hope to build a better world without improving individuals. We all must work for our own improvement, and at the same time share a general responsibility for all humanity.

**Marie Curie, Nobel prize-winning physical chemist**

It must have involved a lot of patience, the admirer remarked. "Everyone has patience," said Paderewski. "I learned to use mine."

**The great pianist and composer, Ignacy Paderewski, was once asked by an admirer how he had reached such a state of perfection in his field.**

The best leaders... almost without exception and at every level, are master users of stories and symbols.

**Tom Peters**

You make more friends by becoming interested in other people than by trying to interest other people in yourself.

**Dale Carnegie**

There are two things to aim at in life : first, to get what you want; and after that to enjoy it. Only the wisest of people achieve the second.

**Logan Pearsall Smith**

Forget the past. Noone BECOMES successful IN the past Love looks through a telescope; envy through a microscope.

**Josh Billings**

If you want children to keep their feet on the ground, put some responsibility on their shoulders.

**Abigail Van Buren**

Leadership is the ability to get people to do what they don't want to do and like it.

**Harry Truman**

You don't strive for sameness, you strive for balance.

**Bear Bryant**

Character is power.

**Booker T. Washington**

Personal gains is empty if you do not feel you have positively touched another's life.

**Barbara Walters**

If you have an important point to make, don't try to be subtle or clever. Use a pile driver. Hit the point once. Then comeback and hit it again. Then hit it a third time a tremendous whack!

**Winston Churchill**

Anyone who angers you conquers you.

**Sister Kenny**

Even on the most exalted throne in the world, you are only sitting on your own bottom.

**Montaigne**

You will never find time for anything. You must make it.

**Charles Buxton**

Satisfaction lies in the effort not the attainment. Full effort is full victory.

**Mahatma Gandhi**

I have learned throughout my life as a composer chiefly through my mistakes and pursuits of false assumptions, not my exposure to founts of wisdom and knowledge.

**Igor Stravinsky**

For the rest of my life I'm going to trust that God is always at work in all things, and give Him thanks long before my simplest prayers are answered.

**Nancy Parker Brummett**

The way I see it, if you want the rainbow, you gotta put up with the rain.

**Dolly Parton**

We must combine the toughness of the serpent and the softness of the dove, a tough mind and a tender heart.

**Martin Luther King, Jr.**

Security is mostly a superstition. It does not exist in nature, nor do the children of men as a whole experience it. Avoiding danger is no safer in the long run than outright exposure. Life is either a daring adventure or nothing.

**Helen Keller (Blinded and deafened by a childhood illness, Helen Keller graduated cum laude from Radcliffe College, and went on to distinguish herself as an author, lecturer and administrator. Her life story was portrayed in the movie, The Miracle Worker.)**

If you can spend a perfectly useless afternoon in a perfectly useless manner, you have learned how to live.

**Lin Yutang**

Grant, Lord, that we might overcome our enemies by transforming them into friends. Make them and make us conscious of those deep inward reaches whereby every heart is rooted in our world's deep common life.

**Jewish Prayer**

Great works are performed not by strength but by perseverance.

**Samuel Johnson**

Today we may face some boring task or idle conversation that feels like a complete waste of time. Perhaps next week or next year we'll understand that nothing is wasted, that in the economy of our universe even a weed is simply a flower whose use has yet to be discovered.

**Mort Crim, Second Thoughts**

It sometimes seems that intense desire creates not only its own opportunities, but its own talents.

**Eric Hoffer**

There is no use whatever trying to help people who do not help themselves. You cannot push anyone up a ladder unless he be willing to climb himself.

**Andrew Carnegie**

Desire! That's the one secret of every man's career. Not education. Not being born with hidden talents. Desire.

**Bobby Unser**

Out of need springs desire, and out of desire springs the energy and the will to win.

**Denis Waitley**

To desire is to obtain; to aspire is to achieve.

**James Allen**

Be careful what you set your heart upon - for it will surely be yours.

**James Baldwin**

We trifle when we assign limits to our desires, since nature hath set none.

**Christian Nevell Bovee**

It sometimes seems that we have only to love a thing greatly to get it.

**Robert Collier**

One essential to success is that your desire be an all obsessing one, your thoughts and aims be co-ordinated, and your energy be concentrated and applied without letup.

**Claude M. Bristol**

The desire not to be anything is the desire not to be.

**Ayn Rand**

The first principle of success is desire - knowing what you want. Desire is the planting of your seed.

**Robert Collier**

Make the iron hot by striking it.

**Oliver Cromwell**

Desire creates the power.

**Raymond Hollingwell**

A desire to be observed, considered, esteemed, praised, beloved, and admired by his fellows is one of the earliest as well as the keenest dispositions discovered in the heart of man.

**John Adams**

You gotta be hungry!

**Les Brown**

Desire, like the atom, is explosive with creative force.

**Paul Vernon Buser**

The battle is all over except the "shouting" when one knows what is wanted and has made up his mind to get it, whatever the price may be.

**Napoleon Hill**

The spirit, the will to win, and the will to excel are the things that endure. These qualities are so much more important than the events that occur.

**Vincent Lombardi**

Zeal is a volcano, the peak of which the grass of indecisiveness does not grow.

**Kahlil Gibran**

It is a funny thing about life; if you refuse to accept anything but the best, you very often get it.

**Somerset Maugham**

When your desires are strong enough you will appear to possess superhuman powers to achieve.

**Napoleon Hill**

Ambition is a dream with a V8 engine.

**Elvis Pressley**

Image creates desire. You will want what you imagine.

**J.G. Gallimore**

Lord, grant that I may always desire more than I can accomplish.

**Michelangelo**

Pearls lie not on the seashore. If thou desirest one thou must dive for it.

**Chinese Proverb**

# *Chapter 2*

Far better it is to dare mighty things, to win glorious triumphs, even though checkered by failure, than to take rank with those poor spirits who neither enjoy nor suffer much, because they live in the gray twilight that knows neither victory nor defeat.

**Theodore Roosevelt**

He who does not enjoy solitude will not love freedom.

**Arthur Schopenhauer**

You can have anything you want if you want it desperately enough. You must want it with an exuberance that erupts through the skin and joins the energy that created the world.

**Sheila Graham**

I'm very determined and stubborn. There's a desire in me that makes me want to do more and more, and to do it right. Each one of us has a fire in our heart for something. It's our goal in life to find it and to keep it.

**Mary Lou Retton**

Some desire is necessary to keep life in motion.

**Samuel Johnson**

Far better it is to dare mightily things, to win glorious triumphs, even though checkered by failure, than to take rank with those poor souls who neither enjoy much nor suffer much, because they live in the gray twilight that knows neither victory nor defeat.

**Theodore Roosevelt**

For what is the best choice, for each individual is the highest it is possible for him to achieve.

**Aristotle**

Desire is the key to motivation, but it's the determination and commitment to an unrelenting pursuit of your goal - a commitment to excellence - that will enable you to attain the success you seek.

**Mario Andretti**

A strong passion... will insure success, for the desire of the end will point out the means.

**Willam Hazlitt**

The starting point of all achievement is desire. Keep this constantly in mind. Weak desire brings weak results, just as a small amount of fire makes a small amount of heat.

**Napoleon Hill**

If you want to succeed, you should strike out on new paths rather than travel the worn paths of accepted success.

**John D. Rockefeller**

Nothing can add more power to your life than concentrating all you energies on a limited set of targets.

**Nido Qubein**

Success is focusing the full power of all you are on what you have a burning desire to achieve.

**Wilferd A. Peterson**

You can have anything you want if you want it badly enough. You can be anything you want to be, do anything you set out to accomplish if you hold to that desire with singleness of purpose.

**Abraham Lincoln**

The mode in which the inevitable comes to pass is through effort.

**Oliver Wendell Holmes**

We are always getting ready to live but never living.

**Ralph Waldo Emerson**

The same hammer that shatters the glass forges the steel.

**Russian Proverb**

A person must stand very tall to see their own fate.

**Danish Proverb**

Thoughts lead on to purposes; purposes go forth in action; actions form habits; habits decide character; and character fixes our destiny.

**Tyron Edwards**

What lies behind us and what lies ahead of us are tiny matters compared to what lives within us.

**Oliver Wendell Holmes**

Every individual has a place to fill in the world, and is important, in some respect, whether he chooses to be so or not.

**Nathaniel Hawthorne**

Control your destiny or somebody else will.

**Jack Welch**

Our first journey is to find that special place for us.

**Earl Nightingale**

There is no such thing as chance; and what seem to us merest accident springs from the deepest source of destiny.

**Johann Friedrich Von Schiller**

The past is like a river flowing out of sight; the future is an ocean filled with opportunity and delight.

**Anna Hoxie**

---

Our problems are man-made, therefore they may be solved by man. No problem of human destiny is beyond human beings.

**John F. Kennedy**

Plan for the future because that's where you are going to spend the rest of your life.

**Mark Twain**

The mind of man is capable of anything because everything is in it, all the past as well as the future.

**Joseph Conrad**

Because your own strength is unequal to the task, do not assume that it is beyond the powers of man; but if anything is within the powers and province of man, believe that it is within your own compass also.

**Marcus Aurelius Antoninus**

No trumpets sound when the important decisions of our life are made. Destiny is made known silently.

**Agnes DeMille**

GOOD is good and bad is bad, and nowhere is the difference between good and bad so wide and so fateful as in human character. For character makes destiny in the individual and in the race.

**Edward O. Sisson**

The purpose of life, after all, is to live it, to taste experience to the utmost, to reach out eagerly and without fear for newer and richer experiences.

**Eleanor Roosevelt**

It is in your moments of decision that your destiny is shaped. Anthony Robbins Ideals are like stars: you will not succeed in touching them with your hands, but like the seafaring man on the ocean desert of waters, you choose them as your guides, and following them, you reach your destiny.

**Carl Schurz**

Hitch your wagon to a star.

**Ralph Waldo Emerson**

Success is not to be pursued; it is to be attracted by the person you become.

**Jim Rohn**

One man scorned and covered with scars still strove with his last ounce of courage to reach the unreachable stars; and the world was better for this.

**Don Quixote**

Character is destiny.

**Heraclitus**

We have no choice of what color we're born or who our parents are or whether we're rich or poor. What we do have is some choice over what we make of our lives once we're here.

**Mildred Taylor**

I don't know what your destiny will be, but one thing I do know; the only ones among you who will be really happy are those who have sought and found how to serve.

**Albert Schweitzer**

There are two educations. One should teach us how to make a living and the other how to live.

**John Adams**

Your profession is not what brings home your paycheck. Your profession is what you were put on earth to do. With such passion and such intensity that it becomes spiritual in calling.

**Vincent Van Gogh**

We are made wise not by the recollection of our past, but by the responsibility for our future.

**George Bernard Shaw**

The great thing in the world is not so much where we stand, as in what direction we are moving.

**Oliver Wendell Holmes**

There are only two ways to live your life. One as though nothing is a miracle. The other is as though everything is a miracle.

**Albert Einstein**

It is a mistake to look too far ahead. Only one link in the chain of destiny can be handled at a time.

**Winston Churchill**

You are today where your thoughts have brought you; you will be tomorrow where your thoughts take you.

**James Allen**

Find something you love to do and you'll never have to work a day in your life.

**Harvey Mackay**

Most people live, whether physically, intellectually or morally, in a very restricted circle of their potential being. They make use of a very small portion of their possible consciousness, and of their soul's resources in general, much like a man who, out of his whole bodily organism, should get into a habit of using and moving only his little finger. Great emergencies and crises show us how much greater our vital resources are than we had supposed.

**William James**

Only complain to someone who can do something about it…Effective complaining helps keep your conversations on the positive side of the street. With some people you may find you have nothing to talk about.

**John-Rogers and Peter McWilliams,
"You Can't Afford the Luxury of a Negative Thought"**

If you don't hurry up and let life know what you want, life will damned soon show you what you'll get.

**Robertson Davies**

Never be in a hurry; do everything quietly and in a calm spirit. Do not lose your inner peace for anything whatsoever, even if your whole world seems upset.

**G. K. Chesterton**

Order marches with weighty and measured strides. Disorder is always in a hurry.

**Napoleon Bonaparte**

Never hurry. Take plenty of exercise. Always be cheerful. Take all the sleep you need. You may expect to be well.

**James Freeman Clarke**

To get all there is out of living, we must employ our time wisely, never being in too much of a hurry to stop and sip life, but never losing our sense of the enormous value of a minute.

**Robert Updegraff**

Chance favors only the prepared mind.

**Louis Pasteur**

Creativity is thinking up new things. Innovation is doing new things.

**Theodore Levitt**

Innovation is the creation of the new or the re-arranging of the old in a new way.

**Michael Vance**

The best way to predict the future is to invent it.

**Alan Kay**

Don't go through life, grow through life.

**Eric Butterworth**

There never was a great soul that did not have some divine inspiration.

**Marcus T. Cicero**

No man can purchase his virtue too dear, for it is the only thing whose value must ever increase with the price it has cost us. Our integrity is never worth so much as when we have parted with our all to keep it.

**Charles Caleb Colton**

My strength is as the strength of ten, because my heart is pure.

**Alfred Lord Tennyson**

Five things constitute perfect virtue: gravity, magnanimity, earnestness, sincerity and kindness.

**Confucius**

No man can tell whether he is rich or poor by turning to his ledger. It is the heart that makes a man rich. He is rich according to what he is, not according to what he has.

**Henry Ward Beecher**

This above all; to thine own self be true.

**William Shakespeare**

The power of man's virtue should not be measured by his special efforts, but by his ordinary doings.

**Blaise Pascal**

Better keep yourself clean and bright. You are the window through which you must see the world.

**George Bernard Shaw**

I have found that being honest is the best technique I can use. Right up front, tell people what you're trying to accomplish and what you're willing to sacrifice to accomplish it.

**Lee Iacocca**

Subtlety may deceive you; integrity never will.

**Oliver Cromwell**

If you have much, give of your wealth; if you have little, give of your heart.

**Arabian Proverb**

Upon the conduct of each depends the fate of all.  Alexander the Great Honesty is the cornerstone of all success, without which confidence and ability to perform shall cease to exist.

**Mary Kay Ash**

I believe that every right implies a responsibility; every opportunity an obligation; every possession a duty.

**John D. Rockefeller**

Good values are easier caught than taught.

**Zig Ziglar**

As we express our gratitude, we must never forget that the highest appreciation is not to utter words, but to live by them.

**John Fitzgerald Kennedy**

Our heritage and ideals, our codes and standards - the things we live by and teach our children - are preserved or diminished by how freely we exchange ideas and feelings.

**Walt Disney**

Live so that when your children think of fairness and integrity, they think of you.

**H. Jackson Brown, Jr.**

A promise must never be broken.

**Alexander Hamilton**

Honor is better than honors.

**Abraham Lincoln**

I had rather do and not promise than promise and not do.

**Arthur Warwick**

Virtue is never left to stand alone. He who has it will have neighbors.

**Confucius**

Moral courage and character go hand in hand... a man of real character is consistently courageous, being imbued with a basic integrity and a firm sense of principle.

**Martha Boaz**

Nothing can harm a good man, either in life or after death.

**Socrates**

The question is not whether we will die, but how we will live.

**Joan Borysenko**

A man, after he has brushed off the dust and chips of his life, will have left only the hard, clean question: Was it good or was it evil? Have I done well - or ill?

**John Steinbeck**

Those who stand for nothing fall for anything.

**Alexander Hamilton**

Honor is like a steep island without a shore: one cannot return once one is outside.

**Nicholas Bouleau**

If it be a sin to covet honor, I am the most offending soul.

**William Shakespeare**

There is no pillow so soft as a clear conscience.

**French Proverb**

In matters of taste, swim with the current. In matters of principle, stand like a rock.

**Thomas Jefferson**

No amount of ability is of the slightest avail without honor.

**Andrew Carnegie**

Good manners will open doors that the best education cannot.

**Clarence Thomas**

I have always tried to be true to myself, to pick those battles I felt were important. My ultimate responsibility is to myself. I could never be anything else.

**Arthur Ashe**

Real integrity is doing the right thing, knowing that nobody's going to know whether you did it or not.

**Oprah Winfrey**

Have no friends not equal to yourself.

**Confucius**

Dignity consists not in possessing honors, but in the consciousness that we deserve them.

**Aristotle**

Contrary to the cliche', genuinely nice guys most often finish first or very near it.

**Malcom S. Forbes**

Whenever you do a thing, act as if all the world were watching.

**Thomas Jefferson**

Rather fall with honor than succeed by fraud.

**Sophocles**

The most important human endeavor is the striving for morality in our actions. Our inner balance, and even our very existence depends on it. Only morality in our actions can give beauty and dignity to our lives.

**Albert Einstein**

Ability will never catch up with the demand for it.

**Malcolm Forbes**

This above all: to thine own self be true, and it must follow, as the night follows day, thou canst not then be false to any man.

**Shakespeare**

If you can not find the truth right where you are, where else do you expect to find it?

**Ralph Waldo Emerson**

What is once well done is done forever.

**Henry David Thoreau**

Always recognize that human individuals are ends, and do not use them as means to your end.

**Immanuel Kant**

Vitality shows not only in the ability to persist, but in the ability to start over.

**F. Scott Fitzgerald**

Don't be sad, don't be angry, if life deceives you!  Submit to your grief -- your time for joy will come, believe me.

**Alexandr Pushkin**

To be somebody, you must last.

**Ruth Gordon**

Ability may get you to the top, but it takes character to keep you there.

**John Wooden**

I was taught that the way of progress is neither swift nor easy.

**Marie Curie**

Self-respect is the root of discipline: The sense of dignity grows with the ability to say no to oneself.

**Abraham Joshua Heschel 1907-1972**

When it is dark enough, you can see the stars.

**Charles A Beard**

All of our dreams can come true -- if we have the courage to pursue them.

**Walt Disney**

Any fact facing us is not as important as our attitude toward it, for that determines our success or failure.

**Norman Vincent Peale**

Care for the small creatures and all else follows.

**Sign at Chicago's Brookfield Zoo**

Never be haughty to the humble; never be humble to the haughty.

**Jefferson Davis (1808-1889)**
**President of the Confederate States of America**

Through perseverance many people win success out of what seemed destined to be certain failure. **Benjamin Disraeli**

Should we feel at times disheartened and discouraged, a confiding thought, a simple movement of heart towards God will renew our powers. Whatever He may demand of us, He will give us at the moment the strength and the courage that we need.

**Francois de la Mothe Fenelon (excerpt from Daily Strengths for Daily Needs by Mary W. Tileston & Claudia Karabaic Sargent)**

Only when one is connected to one's inner core is one connected to others. And, for me, the core, the inner spring, can best be re-found through solitude.

**Anne Morrow Lindbergh**

Each of us owes it to our spouse, our children, our friends, to be as happy as we can be. And if you don't believe me, ask a child what it's like to grow up with an unhappy parent, or ask parents what they suffer if they have an unhappy child.

**Dennis Prager, Happiness is a Serious Problem**

Consult not your fears but your hopes and your dreams. Think not about your frustrations, but about your unfulfilled potential.  Concern yourself not with what you tried and failed in, but with what it is still possible for you to do.

**Pope John XXIII**

One of the things that makes God different from people is that God is always available to listen.

**Rabbi David Wolpe**

The last dejected effort often becomes the winning stroke.

**W.J. Camero**

Today I live in the quiet, joyous expectation of good.

**Ernest Holmen**

Have faith in your dreams and someday Your rainbow will come shining through. No matter how your heart is grieving, if you keep believing the dream that you wish will come true.

**Cinderella**

It is funny about life: if you refuse to accept anything but the very best you will very often get it.

**W. Somerset Maugham**

The timid and fearful first failures dismay, but the stout heart stays trying by night and by day. He values his failures as lessons that teach the one way to get to the goal he would reach.

**Edgar A. Guest**

It's impossible to reach good conclusions with bad information…We're all entitled to our own opinions. But none of us can afford to be wrong in our facts.

**Mort Crim**


Yes, we are all different. Different customs, different foods, different mannerisms, different languages, but not so different that we cannot get along with one another. If we will disagree without being disagreeable.

**J. Martin Kohe**


If we want a free and peaceful world, if we want to make the deserts bloom and man grow to greater dignity as a human being -- we can do it.

**Eleanor Roosevelt**


The mountain remains unmoved at seeming defeat by the mist.

**Rabindranath Tagore**


Courage is resistance to fear, mastery of fear -- not absence of fear. Except a creature be part coward it is not a compliment to say it is brave.

**Mark Twain**

"Happiness"

# *Chapter 3*

Trusting your intuition means tuning in as deeply as you can to the energy you feel, following that energy moment to moment, trusting that it will lead you where you want to go and bring you everything you desire.

**Shakti Gawain**

When your bow is broken and your last arrow spent, then shoot, shoot with your whole heart.

**Zen Saying**

There is no way to peace. Peace is the way.

**A. J. Muste**

A wise old owl sat upon an oak; The more he saw the less he spoke; The less he spoke the more he heard; Why aren't we like that wise old bird?

**Edward Hersey Richards**

Blessed is he who speaks a kindness; thrice blessed is he who repeats it.

**Arabian proverb**

I try to avoid looking forward or backward, and try to keep looking upward.

**Charlotte Bronte**

A community is like a ship; everyone ought to be prepared to take the helm.

**Henrik Ibsen**

The strongest man in the world is he who stands alone.

**Henrik Ibsen**

Few rich men own their own property. The property owns them.

**Robert G. Ingersoll**

The will to win is worthless if you don't get paid for it.

**Reggie Jackson**

It is only when they go wrong that machines remind you how powerful they are.

**Clive James**

A great many people think they are thinking when they are merely rearranging their prejudices.

**William James**

The deepest principle in human nature is the craving to be appreciated.

**William James**

In every country and every age, the priest had been hostile to Liberty.

**Thomas Jefferson**

That government is best which governs least.

**Thomas Jefferson**

It is always the best policy to tell the truth, unless, of course,  you are an exceptionally good liar.

**Jerome K. Jerome**

All riches have their origin in mind. Wealth is in ideas - not money.

**Robert Collier**

Joy is but the sign that creative emotion is fulfilling its purpose.

**Charles Du Bos**

Creative minds have always been known to survive any kind of bad training.

**Anna Freud**

Making the simple complicated is commonplace; making the complicated simple, awesomely simple, that's creative.

**Charles Mingus**

To think creatively, we must be able to look afresh at what we normally take for granted.

**George Kneller**

Dig within. Within is the wellspring of good; and it is always ready to bubble up, if you just dig.

**Marcus Aurelius**

The only limits are, as always, those of vision.

**James Broughton**

Those who wish to sing, always find a song.

**Swedish Proverb**

Light tomorrow with today.

**Elizabeth Barrett Browning**

A will finds a way.

**Orison Swett Marsden**

A new idea is delicate. It can be killed by a sneer or a yawn; it can be stabbed to death by a quip and worried to death by a frown on the right man's brow.

**Charles Brower**

There are painters who transform the sun to a yellow spot, but there are others who with the help of their art and their intelligence, transform a yellow spot into the sun.

**Pablo Picasso**

Any activity becomes creative when the doer cares about doing it right, or better.

**John Updike**

You cannot step twice into the same river; for other waters are continually flowing in.

**Heraclitus**

We are not creatures of circumstance; we are creators of circumstance.

**Benjamin Disraeli**

There is a boundary to men's passions when they act from feelings; but none when they are under the influence of imagination.

**Edmund Burke**

If I have seen farther than others, it is because I was standing on the shoulders of giants.

**Isaac Newton**

Feeling and longing are the motive forces behind all human endeavor and human creations.

**Albert Einstein**

To exist is to change, to change is to mature, to mature is to go on creating oneself endlessly.

**Henri L Bergson**

Happiness is not in the mere possession of money; it lies in the joy of achievement, in the thrill of creative effort.

**Franklin Roosevelt**

An idea not coupled with action will never get any bigger than the brain cell it occupied.

**Arnold Glascow**

An avalanche begins with a snowflake.

**Joseph Compton**

To me, the greatest pleasure of writing is not what it's about, but the inner music that words make.

**Truman Capote**

The ability to convert ideas to things is the secret of outward success.

**Henry Ward Beecher**

The significant problems we face cannot be solved at the same level of thinking we were at when we created them.

**Albert Einstein**

The mind is its own place, and in itself, can make heaven of Hell, and a hell of Heaven.

**John Milton**

Creativity is thinking up new things. Innovation is doing new things.

**Theodore Levitt**

When you cannot make up your mind which of two evenly balanced courses of action you should take - choose the bolder.

**William Joseph Slim**

Indecision is debilitating; it feeds upon itself; it is, one might almost say, habit-forming. Not only that, but it is contagious; it transmits itself to others.

**H. A. Hopf**

We choose our joys and sorrows long before we experience them.

**Kahlil Gibran**

When making a decision of minor importance, I have always found it advantageous to consider all the pros and cons. In vital matters, however, such as the choice of a mate or a profession, the decision should come from the unconscious, from somewhere within ourselves. In the important decisions of personal life, we should be governed, I think, by the deep inner needs of our nature.

**Sigmund Freud**

We know what happens to people who stay in the middle of the road. They get run over.

**Aneurin Bevan**

Whenever you see a successful business, someone once made a courageous decision.

**Peter Drucker**

Nothing is more difficult, and therefore more precious, than to be able to decide.

**Napoleon Bonaparte**

When you have to make a choice and you don't make it, that itself is a choice.

**William James**

Choose always the way that seems the best, however rough it may be. Custom will soon render it easy and agreeable.

**Pythagoras**

'Do somethings' are not moved by the criticism of 'do nothings'.

**Peter Sinclair**

Vacillating people seldom succeed. Successful men and women are very careful in reaching their decisions, and very persistent and determined in action thereafter.

**L. G. Elliott**

In a moment of decision, the best thing you can do is the right thing to do. The worst thing you can do is nothing.

**Theodore Roosevelt**

Once you make a decision, the universe conspires to make it happen.

**Ralph Waldo Emerson**

There is no more miserable human being than one in whom nothing is habitual but indecision.

**William James**

Successful leaders have the courage to take action while others hesitate.

**John C. Maxwell**

One thing is sure. We have to do something. We have to do the best we know how at the moment...;If it doesn't turn out right, we can modify it as we go along.

**Franklin D. Roosevelt**

Please all, and you will please none.

**Aesop**

By three methods we may learn wisdom: First, by reflection, which is noblest; Second, imitation, which is easiest; and third by experience, which is the bitterest.

**Confucius**

It's not hard to make decisions when you know what your values are.

**Roy Disney**

---

Confidence is the result of hours and days and weeks and years of constant work and dedication.

**Roger Staubach**

We all have dreams. But in order to make dreams come into reality, it takes an awful lot of determination, dedication, self-discipline, and effort.

**Jesse Owens**

Determine what specific goal you want to achieve. Then dedicate yourself to its attainment with unswerving singleness of purpose, the trenchant zeal of a crusader.

**Paul J. Meyer**

Men are like wine - some turn to vinegar, but the best improve with age.

**Pope John XXIII**

Patriotism is the last refuge of the scoundrel.

**Samuel Johnson**

An ounce of emotion is equal to a ton of facts.

**John Junor**

In the fight between you and the world, back the world.

**Franz Kafka**

You do not destroy an idea by killing people; you replace it with a better one.

**Edward Keating**

College isn't the place to go for ideas.

**Helen Keller**

Science may have found a cure for most evils;  but it has found no remedy for the worst of them all- the apathy of human beings.

**Helen Keller**

Mankind must put an end to war, or war will put an end to mankind.

**John F. Kennedy**

If a free society cannot help the many who are poor, it cannot save the few who are rich.

**John F. Kennedy**

Those who make peaceful revolution impossible will make violent revolution inevitable.

**John F. Kennedy**

We have the power to make this the best generation of mankind in the history of the world - or to make it the last.

**John F. Kennedy**

And so, my fellow Americans, ask not what your country can do for you;  ask what you can do for your country.

**John F. Kennedy**

Only those who dare to fail greatly can ever achieve greatly.

**Robert F. Kennedy**

Not the owner of many possessions will you be right to call happy: he more rightly deserves the name of happy who knows how to use the Gods' gifts wisely and to put up with rough poverty, and who fears dishonor more than death.

**Horace (65-8 BC) Roman Poet**

In the long run we are all dead.

**John Maynard Keynes**

---

Politicians are the same all over.  They promise to build bridges even when there are no rivers.

**Nikita Khruschev**

Injustice anywhere is a threat to justice everywhere.

**Martin Luther King Jr.**

The ultimate measure of a man is not where he stands in moments of comfort, but where he stands at times of challenge and controversy.

**Martin Luther King Jr.**

Words are, of course, the most powerful drug used by mankind.

**Rudyard Kipling**

The illegal we do immediately. The unconstitutional takes a little longer.

**Henry Kissinger**

Television - a medium. So called because it is neither rare nor well-done.

**Ernie Kovacs**

Pick battles big enough to matter, small enough to win.

**Jonathan Kozol**

People don't ask for facts in making up their minds.  They would rather have one good, soul-satisfying emotion than a dozen facts.

**Robert Keith Leavitt**

Physics isn't a religion. If it were, we'd have a much easier time raising money.

**Leon Lederman**

If you rest, you rust.

**Helen Keller**

It's not than I'm so smart, it's just that I stay with problems longer.

**Albert Einstein**

Wheresoever you go, go with all your heart.

**Confucius**

If you are truly flexible and go until... there is really very little you can't accomplish in your lifetime.

**Anthony Robbins**

To have striven, to have made the effort, to have been true to certain ideals - this alone is worth the struggle.

**Sir William Osler**

Do not quit! Hundreds of times I have watched people throw in the towel at the one-yard line while someone else comes along and makes a fortune by just going that extra yard.

**E. Joseph Cossman**

Losers make promises they often break. Winners make commitments they always keep.

**Denis Waitley**

The freedom to be your best means nothing unless you are willing to do your best.

**Colin Powell**

To avoid criticism, do nothing, say nothing, be nothing.

**Elbert Hubbard**

A promise must never be broken.

**Alexander Hamilton**

The successful person has the habit of doing the things failures don't like to do. They don't like doing them either necessarily. But their disliking is subordinated to the strength of their purpose.

**E.M. Gray**

Most of us serve our ideals by fits and starts. The person who makes a success of living is one who sees his goal steadily and aims for it unswervingly. That's dedication.

**Cecil B. DeMille**

It's amazing what ordinary people can do if they set out without preconceived notions.

**Charles Kettering**

I know the price of success: dedication, hard work, and an unremitting devotion to the things you want to see happen.

**Frank Lloyd Wright**

There's no scarcity of opportunity to make a living at what you love. There is only a scarcity of resolve to make it happen.

**Wayne Dyer**

When firmness is sufficient, rashness is unnecessary.

**Napoleon Bonaparte**

Don't compromise yourself. You are all you've got.

**Janis Joplin**

The best way to predict the future is to invent it.

**Alan Kay**

You may have to fight a battle more than once to win it.

**Margaret Thatcher**

If you hear a voice within you say 'you cannot paint,' then by all means paint and that voice will be silenced.

**Vincent Van Gogh**

You cannot shake hands with a clenched fist.

**Indira Gandhi**

Any activity becomes creative when the doer cares about doing it right, or doing it better.

**John Updike**

Decide that you want it more than you are afraid of it.

**Bill Cosby**

My advice is to go into something and stay with it until you like it. You can't like it until you obtain expertise in that work. And once you are an expert, it's a pleasure.

**Milton Garland**

A successful life doesn't require that we've done the best, but that we've done our best.

**H. Jackson Brown**

A man's word and his intestinal fortitude are two of the most honorable virtues known to mankind.

**Jim Nantz**

Twenty years from now you will be more disappointed by the things that you didn't do than by the ones you did so. So throw off the bowlines. Sail away from the safe harbor. Catch the trade winds in your sails. Explore. Dream. Discover.

**Mark Twain**

The will to win, the desire to succeed, the urge to reach your full potential... these are the keys that will unlock the door to personal excellence.

**Eddie Robinson**

Stand up to your obstacles and do something about them. You will find that they haven't half the strength you think they have.

**Norman Vincent Peale**

Good is not good where better is expected.

**Thomas Fuller**

Try not to become a man of success, but rather to become a man of value. He is considered successful in our day who gets more out of life than he puts in. But a man of value will give more than he receives.

**Albert Einstein**

What this power is I cannot say; all I know is that it exists and it becomes available only when a man is in that state of mind in which he knows exactly what he wants and is fully determined not to quit until he finds it.

**Alexander Graham Bell**

Make the most of yourself, for that is all there is of you.

**Ralph Waldo Emerson**

Life is not holding a good hand; life is playing a poor hand well.

**Danish proverb**

Most of the important things in the world have been accomplished by people who have kept on trying when there seemed to be no hope at all.

**Dale Carnegie**

One worthwhile task carried to a successful conclusion is worth half-a-hundred half-finished tasks.

**Malcom S. Forbes**

A man who won't die for something is not fit to live.

**Martin Luther King, Jr.**

Make each day your masterpiece.

**John Wooden**

Effort only fully releases its reward after a person refuses to quit.

**Napoleon Hill**

The harder you work, the harder it is to surrender.

**Vincent Lombardi**

When I'd get tired and want to stop. I'd wonder what my next opponent was doing. I'd wonder if he was still working out. I tried to visualize him. When I could see him still working, I'd start pushing myself. When I could see him quit, I'd push myself harder.

**Dan Gable**

You cannot do a kindness too soon, for you never know how soon it will be too late.

**Ralph Waldo Emerson**

It is necessary to the happiness of man that he be mentally faithful to himself.

**Thomas Paine**

When you get in a tight place and everything goes against you, till it seems as though you could not hold on a minute longer, never give up then, for that is just the place and time that the tide will turn.

**Harriott Beecher Stowe**

Always dream and shoot higher than you know how to. Don't bother just to be better than your contemporaries or predecessors. Try to be better than yourself.

**William Faulkner**

The question in life is not whether you get knocked down. You will. The question is, are you ready to get back up ... and fight for what you believe in?

**Dan Quayle**

It is not because things are difficult that we do not dare. It is because we do not dare that things are difficult.

**Seneca**

Strength is a matter of the made-up mind.

**John Beecher**

Do all the good you can By all the means you can In all the ways you can In all the places you can At all the times you can To all the people you can As long as ever you can.

**John Wesley**

Smooth seas do not make skillful sailors.

**African Proverb**

The greatest thing in the world is not so much where we are, but in what direction we are moving.

**Oliver Wendell Holmes**

The greatest glory in living lies not in never falling, but in rising every time we fall.

**Nelson Mandella**

All right Mister, let me tell you what winning means...you're willing to go longer, work harder, give more than anyone else.

**Vincent Lombardi**

When written in Chinese the word crisis is composed to two characters. One represents danger, and the other represents opportunity.

**John F. Kennedy**

Perseverance is failing 19 times and succeeding the 20th.

**Julie Andrews**

We all have ability. The difference is how we use it.

**Stevie Wonder**

You are the only person on earth who can use your ability.

**Zig Ziglar**

No amount of ability is of the slightest avail without honor.

**Andrew Carnegie**

Big jobs usually go to the men who prove their ability to outgrow small ones.

**Ralph Waldo Emerson**

The real contest is always between what you've done and what you're capable of doing. You measure yourself against yourself and nobody else.

**Geoffrey Gaberino**

Natural ability without education has more often raised a man to glory and virtue than education without natural ability.

**Marcus T. Cicero**

Put yourself in a state of mind where you say to yourself, "Here is an opportunity for me to celebrate like never before, my own power, my own ability to get myself to do whatever is necessary.

**Tony Robbins**

The world cares very little about what a man or woman knows; it is what a man or woman is able to do that counts.

**Booker T. Washington**

You are searching for the magic key that will unlock the door to the source of power; and yet you have the key in your own hands, and you may use it the moment you learn to control your thoughts.

**Napoleon Hill**

Life is a field of unlimited possibilities.

**Deepak Chopra**

Everything you need you already have. You are complete right now, you are a whole, total person, not an apprentice person on the way to someplace else. Your completeness must be understood by you and experienced in your thoughts as your own personal reality.

**Wayne Dyer**

You must be careful how you walk, and where you go, for there are those following you who will set their feet where yours are set.

**Robert E. Lee**

The abundant life does not come to those who have had a lot of obstacles removed from their path by others. It develops from within and is rooted in strong mental and moral fiber.

**William Mather Lewis**

# Chapter 4

Not what we have But what we enjoy, constitutes our abundance.

**John Petit-Senn**

My mother drew a distinction between achievement and success. She said that achievement is the knowledge that you have studied and worked hard and done the best that is in you. Success is being praised by others. That is nice but not as important or satisfying. Always aim for achievement and forget about success.

**Helen Hayes**

High achievement always takes place in the framework of high expectation.

**Jack Kinder**

I feel that the greatest reward for doing is the opportunity to do more.

**Dr. Jonas Salk**

Winners take time to relish their work, knowing that scaling the mountain is what makes the view from the top so exhilarating.

**Denis Waitley**

The roots of true achievement lie in the will to become the best that you can become.

**Harold Taylor**

I have the simplest tastes. I am always satisfied with the best.

**Oscar Wilde**

Think of yourself as on the threshold of unparalleled success. A whole clear, glorious life lies before you. Achieve! Achieve!

**Andrew Carnegie**

The man who does things makes many mistakes, but he never makes the biggest mistake of all - doing nothing.

**Benjamin Franklin**

The quality, not the longevity, of one's life is what is important.

**Martin Luther King, Jr.**

It is well that war is so terrible, or we should get too fond of it.

**Robert E. Lee**

There is a terrible war coming, and these young men who have never seen war cannot wait for it to happen, but I tell you, I wish that I owned every slave in the South, for I would free them all to avoid this war.

**Robert E. Lee**

It is true that liberty is precious - so precious that it must be rationed.

**Nikolai Lenin**

The world began without man, and it will complete itself without him.

**Claude Levi-Strauss**

He who is plenteously provided for from within, needs but little from without.

**Johann Wolfgang Von Goethe**

The education of a man is never completed until he dies.

**Robert E. Lee**

Statistics are like a bikini. What they reveal is suggestive, but what they conceal is vital.

**Aaron Levenstein**

Ask a man which way he is going to vote, and he will probably tell you. Ask him, however, why, and vagueness is all.

**Bernard Levin**

Our doubts are traitors and make us lose the good we might win, by fearing to attempt.

**William Shakespeare**

The fearful unbelief is unbelief in yourself.

**Thomas Carlyle**

Philosophy when superficially studied, excites doubt, when thoroughly explored, it dispels it.

**Francis Bacon**

When in doubt, don't.

**Benjamin Franklin**

Doubt is a pain too lonely to know that faith is his twin brother.

**Kahlil Gibran**

There was a castle called Doubting Castle, the owner whereof was Giant Despair.

**John Bunyan**

Doubt is the vestibule through which all must pass before they can enter into the temple of wisdom.

**Colton**

Doubt whom you will, but never yourself.

**Christian N. Bovee**

The only limit to our realization of tomorrow will be our doubts about reality.

**Franklin Delano Roosevelt**

Jealousy lives upon doubts, it becomes madness or ceases entirely as soon as we pass from doubt to certainty.

**Francois de La Rochefoucauld**

---

The trouble with the world is that the stupid are cocksure and the intelligent full of doubt.

**Bertrand Russell**

If a man will begin with certainties, he shall end in doubts; but if he will be content to begin with doubts, he shall end in certainties.

**Francis Bacon**

Failure is in a sense the highway to success, as each discovery of what is false leads us to seek earnestly after what is true.

**John Keats**

We don't grow unless we take risks. Any successful company is riddled with failures.

**James E. Burke**

To begin to think with purpose, is to enter the ranks of those strong ones who only recognize failure as one of the pathways to attainment.

**James Allen**

The only true failure lies in failure to start.

**Harold Blake Walker**

Don't be afraid to fail. Don't waste energy trying to cover up failure. Learn from your failures and go on to the next challenge. It's OK to fail. If you're not failing, you're not growing.

**H. Stanley Judd**

Failures are like skinned knees, painful but superficial.

**H. Ross Perot**

The difference between failure and success is doing a thing nearly right and doing it exactly right.

**Edward Simmons**

Fear of failure must never be a reason not to try something.

**Frederick Smith**

The person interested in success has to learn to view failure as a healthy, inevitable part of the process of getting to the top.

**Dr. Joyce Brothers**

Forget about the consequences of failure. Failure is only a temporary change in direction to set you straight for your next success.

**Denis Waitley**

My great concern is not whether you have failed, but whether you are content with your failure.

**Abraham Lincoln**

Persistent people begin their success where others end in failure.

**Edward Eggleston**

I am not discouraged, because every wrong attempt discarded is another step forward.

**Thomas A. Edison**

The way to succeed is to double your failure rate.

**Thomas Watson**

History has demonstrated that the most notable winners usually encountered heartbreaking obstacles before they triumphed. They won because they refused to become discouraged by their defeats.

**B. C. Forbes**

Stumbling is not falling.

**Portuguese Proverb**

Gray skies are just clouds passing over.

**Duke Ellington**

You always pass failure on the way to success.

**Mickey Rooney**

You may have a fresh start any moment you choose, for this thing that we call 'failure' is not the falling down, but the staying down.

**Mary Pickford**

An inventor fails 999 times, and if he succeeds once, he's in. He treats his failures simply as practice shots.

**Charles Kettering**

Whenever I hear anyone arguing for slavery, I feel a strong impulse to see it tried on him personally.

**Abraham Lincoln**

Being challenged in life is inevitable, being defeated is optional.

**Roger Crawford**

Failure is the condiment that gives success its flavor.

**Truman Capote**

Recovering from failure is often easier than building from success.

**Michael Eisner**

A stumble may prevent a fall.

**English proverb**

Failure is an event, never a person; an attitude, not an outcome.

**Zig Ziglar**

Don't be discouraged by failure. It can be a positive experience. Failure is, in a sense, the highway to success, inasmuch as every discovery of what is false leads us to seek earnestly after what is true, and every fresh experience points out some form of error which we shall afterwards carefully avoid.

**John Keats**

Never confuse a single defeat with a final defeat.

**F. Scott Fitzgerald**

Failure doesn't mean that you're a failure ... it just means that you haven't succeeded yet.

**Robert Schuler**

Develop success from failures. Discouragement and failure are two of the surest stepping stones to success.

**Dale Carnegie**

When you make a mistake or get ridiculed or rejected, look at mistakes as learning experiences, and ridicule as ignorance. Look at rejection as part of one performance, not as a turn down of the performer.

**Denis Waitley**

You're never beaten until you admit it.

**George S. Patton**

You become strong by defying defeat and by turning loss into gain and failure to success.

**Napoleon**

Failure is a detour, not a dead end street.

**Zig Ziglar**

Nearly all men can stand adversity, but if you want to test a man's character, give him power.

**Abraham Lincoln**

You can fool all the people some of the time, and some of the people all the time, but you cannot fool all the people all the time.

**Abraham Lincoln**

Good communication is as stimulating as black coffee, and just as hard to sleep after.

**Anne Morrow Lindbergh**

Where all men think alike, no one thinks very much.

**Walter Lippmann**

I have always thought the actions of men the best interpreters of their thoughts.

**John Locke**

Winning is not everything. It's the only thing.

**Vince Lombardi**

Everybody wants to go to heaven, but nobody wants to die.

**Joe Louis**

In war there is no substitute for victory.

**General Douglas MacArthur**

It is much more secure to be feared than to be loved.

**Niccolo Machiavelli**

All our knowledge merely helps us to die a more painful death than animals that know nothing.

**Maurice Maeterlinck**

---

Politics is war without bloodshed while war is politics with bloodshed.

**Mao Zedong**

An optimist is a guy that has never had much experience.

**Donald R. Perry Marquis**

From each according to his abilities, to each according to his needs.

**Karl Marx**

Religion... is the opium of the masses.

**Karl Marx**

Love is only the dirty trick played on us to achieve continuation of the species.

**W. Somerset Maugham**

A politician is an animal which can sit on a fence and yet keep both ears to the ground. Love is the triumph of imagination over intelligence. No one ever went broke underestimating the taste of the American public. Time is the great legalizer, even in the field of morals. The older I grow the more I distrust the familiar doctrine that age brings wisdom. Conscience is the inner voice that warns us that someone might be looking.

**H. L. Mencken**

A good listener is not only popular everywhere,  but after a while he gets to know something.

**Wilson Mizner**

When you take stuff from one writer it's plagiarism;  but when you take it from many writers, it's research.

**Wilson Mizner**

Gambling: The sure way of getting nothing for something.

**Wilson Mizner**

Obstacles are those frightful things you see when you take your eyes off the goal.

**Hannah More**

You have not converted a man because you have silenced him.

**John Morley**

Any party which takes credit for the rain must not be surprised if its opponents blame it for the drought.

**Dwight Morrow**

It's so easy to laugh. It's so easy to hate. It takes strength to be gentle and kind.

**Stephen Morrissey**

Anyone who isn't confused really doesn't understand the situation.

**Edward R. Murrow**

Nothing is more effective than sincere, accurate praise, and nothing is more lame than a cookie-cutter compliment.

**Bill Walsh**

At times our own light goes out and is rekindled by a spark from another person. Each of us has cause to think with deep gratitude of those who have lighted the flame within us.

**Albert Schweitzer**

Appreciation can make a day, even change a life. Your willingness to put it into words is all that is necessary.

**Margaret Cousins**

Habit is second nature, or rather, ten times nature.

**William James**

We first make our habits, and then our habits make us.

**John Dryden**

First we form habits, then they form us. Conquer your bad habits, or they'll eventually conquer you.

**Dr. Rob Gilbert**

Your net worth to the world is usually determined by what remains after your bad habits are subtracted from your good ones.

**Benjamin Franklin**

Habits are at first cobwebs, then cables.

**Spanish Proverb**

The chains of habit are generally too small to be felt until they are too strong to be broken.

**Samuel Johnson**

Habit is habit and not to be flung out of the window by any man, but coaxed downstairs a step at a time.

**Mark Twain**

Man becomes a slave to his constantly repeated acts. What he at first chooses, at last compels.

**Orison Swett Marsden**

Once you learn to quit, it becomes a habit.

**Vincent Lombardi**

Habit is either the best of servants or the worst of masters.

**Nathaniel Emmons**

Winning is a habit. Unfortunately, so is losing.

**Vincent Lombardi**

---

Motivation is what gets you started. Habit is what keeps you going.

**Jim Ryun**

Choose the life that is most useful, and habit will make it the most agreeable.

**Francis Bacon**

Start each day by affirming peaceful, contented and happy attitudes and your days will tend to be pleasant and successful.

**Norman Vincent Peale**

Very little is needed to make a happy life; it is all within yourself, in your way of thinking.

**Marcus Aurelius**

A happy person is not a person in a certain set of circumstances, but rather a person with a certain set of attitudes.

**Hugh Downs**

No one can be great, or good, or happy except through the inward efforts of themselves.

**Frederick W. Robertson**

Cherish all your happy moments; they make a fine cushion for old age.

**Booth Tarkington**

Whoever is happy will make others happy too.

**Anne Frank**

Happiness is a direction, not a place.

**Sydney J. Harris**

The good life, as I conceive it, is a happy life. I do not mean that if you are good you will be happy; I mean that if you are happy you will be good.

**Bertrand Russell**

Joy is not in things; it is in us.

**John Wagner**

The Constitution only gives people the right to pursue happiness. You have to catch it yourself.

**Benjamin Franklin**

The grand essentials of happiness are: something to do, something to love, and something to hope for.

**Allan K. Chalmers**

Remember this - very little is needed to make a happy life.

**Marcus Aurelius**

If you want happiness for an hour, take a nap. If you want happiness for a day, go fishing. If you want happiness for a year, inherit a fortune. If you want happiness for a lifetime, help somebody.

**Chinese Proverb**

The foolish man seeks happiness in the distance; The wise grow it under his feet.

**James Oppenheim**

Happiness does not depend on what happens outside of you but on what happens inside of you; it is measured by the spirit with which you meet the problems of life.

**Harold B. Lee**

Happiness makes up in height what it lacks in length.

**Robert Frost**

Happiness is man's greatest aim in life. Tranquility and rationality are the cornerstones of happiness.

**Epicurus**

It is the chiefest point of happiness that a man is willing to be what he is.

**Desiderius Erasmus**

Happiness is perfume you can't pour on others without getting a few drops for yourself.

**Ralph Waldo Emerson**

Success is getting what you want, happiness is wanting what you get.

**Dave Gardner**

I believe that unarmed truth and unconditional love will have the final word in reality. That is why right, temporarily defeated, is stronger than evil triumphant.

**Martin Luther King, Jr.**

To attain happiness in another world we need only to believe something, while to secure it in this world we must do something.

**C.P. Gilman**

Happiness often sneaks through a door you didn't know you left open.

**John Barrymore**

Happiness is the real sense of fulfillment that comes from hard work.

**Joseph Barbara**

To have joy one must share it. Happiness was born a twin.

**Lord Byron**

But what is happiness except the simple harmony between a man and the life he leads?

**Albert Camus**

Just play. Have fun. Enjoy the game.

**Michael Jordan**

Think of all the beauty still left around you and be happy.

**Anne Frank**

The secret of happiness is something to do.

**John Burroughs**

Happiness in this world, when it comes, comes incidentally. Make it the object of pursuit, and it leads us a wild-goose chase, and is never attained. Follow some other object, and very possibly we may find that we have caught happiness without dreaming of it.

**Nathaniel Hawthorne**

It makes no difference where you go, there you are. And it makes no difference what you have, there's always more to want. Until you are happy with who you are, you will never be happy because of what you have.

**Zig Ziglar**

Happiness cannot be traveled to, owned, earned, worn or consumed. Happiness is the spiritual experience of living every minute with love, grace and gratitude.

**Denis Waitley**

Happiness depends upon ourselves.

**Aristotle**

You are forgiven for your happiness and your successes only if you generously consent to share them.

**Albert Camus**

Happiness is a state of activity.

**Aristotle**

---

The foolish man seeks happiness in the distance; the wise grows it under his feet.

**James Oppenheim**

People take different roads seeking fulfillment and happiness. Just because they're not on your road doesn't mean they've gotten lost.

**H. Jackson Brown, Jr.**

He is happiest, be he king or peasant, who finds peace in his home.

**Johann von Goethe**

The best way to cheer yourself up is to try to cheer somebody else up.

**Mark Twain**

The more you praise and celebrate your life, the more there is in life to celebrate.

**Oprah Winfrey**

Happiness is a butterfly, which, when pursued, is always just beyond your grasp, but which, if you will sit down quietly, may alight upon you.

**Nathaniel Hawthorne**

Many persons have the wrong idea of what constitutes true happiness. It is not attained through self-gratification but through fidelity to a worthy purpose.

**Helen Keller**

The most wasted of all days is one without laughter.

**E.E. Cummings**

I live by this credo: Have a little laugh at life and look around you for happiness instead of sadness. Laughter has always brought me out of unhappy situations. Even in your darkest moment, you usually can find something to laugh about if you try hard enough.

**Red Skelton**

# *Chapter 5*

---

Happiness is that state of consciousness which proceeds from the achievement of one's values.

**Ayn Rand**

A man is happy so long as he chooses to be happy.

**Alexander Solzhenitsyn**

Happiness is the meaning and the purpose of life, the whole aim and end of human existence.

**Aristotle**

Did you ever see an unhappy horse? Did you ever see bird that had the blues? One reason why birds and horses are not unhappy is because they are not trying to impress other birds and horses.

**Dale Carnegie**

A light heart lives long.

**William Shakespeare**

Laughter is inner jogging.

**Norman Cousins**

Laughter is the sun that drives winter from the human face.

**Victor Hugo**

A laugh is the shortest distance between two people.

**Victor Borge**

The happiness of your life depends upon the quality of your thoughts... take care that you entertain no notions unsuitable to virtue and reasonable nature.

**Marcus Aurelius**

---

There is only one way to happiness, and that is cease worrying about the things which are beyond the power of our will.

**Epictetus**

Until you are happy with who you are, you will never be happy with what you have.

**Zig Ziglar**

No one has a right to consume happiness without producing it.

**Helen Keller**

I've learned from experience that the greater part of our happiness or misery depends on our dispositions and not on our circumstances.

**Martha Washington**

Three grand essentials to happiness in this life are something to do, something to love and something to hope for.

**Joseph Addison**

Happiness is a by-product of an effort to make someone else happy.

**Gretta Brooker Palmer**

Action may not always bring happiness, but there is no happiness without action.

**Benjamin Disraeli**

Happiness lies in the joy of achievement and the thrill of creative effort.

**Franklin D. Roosevelt**

Even if happiness forgets you a little bit, never completely forget about it.

**Jacques Prévert**

Different men seek after happiness in different ways and by different means, and so make for themselves different modes of life and forms of government.

**Aristotle**

Meditate. Live purely. Be quiet. Do your work with mastery. Like the moon, come out from behind the clouds! Shine.

**Buddha**

Dedicate yourself to the good you deserve and desire for yourself. Give yourself peace of mind. You deserve to be happy. You deserve delight.

**Mark Victor Hansen**

If you never did, you should. These things are fun, and fun is good.

**Dr. Seuss**

People rarely succeed unless they have fun in what they are doing.

**Dale Carnegie**

Man needs, for his happiness, not only the enjoyment of this or that, but hope and enterprise and change.

**Bertrand Russell**

Happiness is not something you postpone for the future; it is something you design for the present.

**Jim Rohn**

Pleasure is the only thing to live for. Nothing ages like happiness.

**Oscar Wilde**

Fun is about as good as a habit as there is.

**Jimmy Buffett**

You're a happy fellow, for you'll give happiness and joy to many other people. There is nothing better or greater than that.

**Ludwig van Beethoven**

The supreme happiness in life is the conviction that we are loved.

**Victor Hugo**

Since you get more joy out of giving joy to others, you should put a good deal of thought into the happiness that you are able to give.

**Eleanor Roosevelt**

Happiness is not a reward - it is consequence. Suffering is not a punishment - it is a result.

**Robert Green Ingersoll**

Happiness is nothing more than good health and a bad memory.

**Albert Schweitzer**

The perfection of wisdom and the end of true philosophy is to proportion our wants to our possessions, our ambitions to our capacities, we will then be a happy and a virtuous people.

**Mark Twain**

I cannot give you the formula for success, but I can give you the formula for failure, which is: try to please everybody.

**Herbert Bayard Swope**

Our problems are man-made, therefore they may be solved by man. No problem of human destiny is beyond human beings.

**John F. Kennedy**

Do not think of your faults; still less of others' faults. Look for what is good and strong and try to imitate it. Your faults will drop off like dead leaves when their time comes.

**John Ruskin**

Nothing in life is to be feared. It is only to be understood.

**Marie Curie**

Don't find fault. Find a remedy.

**Henry Ford**

The important thing is not to stop questioning.

**Albert Einstein**

Happiness does not come from doing easy work but from the afterglow of satisfaction that comes after the achievement of a difficult task that demanded our best.

**Theodore Rubin**

Nobody is bored when he is trying to make something that is beautiful, or to discover something that is true.

**William Inge**

The "how" thinker gets problems solved effectively because he wastes no time with futile "ifs" but goes right to work on the creative "how".

**Norman Vincent Peale**

When I dig another out of trouble, the hole from which I lift him is the place where I bury my own.

**Norman Vincent Peale**

We are at our very best, and we are happiest, when we are fully engaged in work we enjoy on the journey toward the goal we've established for ourselves. It gives meaning to our time off and comfort to our sleep. It makes everything else in life so wonderful, so worthwhile.

**Earl Nightingale**

Every single one of us can do things that no one else can do - can love things that no one else can love. We are like violins. We can be used for doorstops, or we can make music. You know what to do.

**Barbara Sher**

Be not simply good; be good for something.

**Henry David Thoreau**

Chase your passion, not your pension.

**Denis Waitley**

The tragedy of life is what dies inside a man while he lives.

**Albert Schweitzer**

We succeed only as we identify in life, or in war, or in anything else, a single overriding objective, and make all other considerations bend to that one objective.

**Dwight D. Eisenhower**

Don't ask yourself what the world needs; ask yourself what makes you come alive. And then go and do that. Because what the world needs are people who have come alive.

**Harold Whitman**

He who has a why to live for can bear almost any how.

**Friedrich Nietzsche**

What mankind wants is not talent; it is purpose.

**Edward G. Bulwer-Lytton**

Cherish your visions; cherish your ideals; cherish the music that stirs in your heart, the beauty that forms in your mind, the loveliness that drapes your purest thoughts, for out of them will grow delightful conditions, all heavenly environment; of these if you but remain true to them, your world will at last be built.

**James Allen**


Look for an occupation that you like, and you will not need to labor for a single day in your life.

**Confucius**


The purpose of life is a life of purpose.

**Robert Byrne**


An aim in life is the only fortune worth finding.

**Jacqueline Kennedy Onassis**


Life isn't about finding yourself. Life is about creating yourself.

**George Bernard Shaw**


Always be a first-rate version of yourself, instead of a second-rate version of somebody else.

**Judy Garland**


We are not here merely to make a living. We are here to enrich the world.

**Woodrow Wilson**

I think about my own death, and I think about my own funeral. And if you get somebody to deliver the eulogy ... tell them not to mention that I have a Nobel Peace Prize ... that I have three or four hundred other awards. I'd like for somebody to say that day that Martin Luther King Jr. tried to give his life serving others.... Say that I was a drum major for justice ... for peace ... for righteousness ... I just want to leave a committed life behind.

**Dr. Martin Luther King, Jr.**

Here is a test to find out whether your mission in life is complete. If you're alive, it isn't.

**Richard Bach**

The first thing is to love your sport. Never do it to please someone else. It has to be yours.

**Peggy Fleming**

Be yourself. The world worships the original.

**Ingrid Bergman**

All of us have at least one great voice deep inside.

**Pat Riley**

The more you loose yourself in something bigger than yourself, the more energy you will have.

**Norman Vincent Peale**

Really think hard about what you want to do, because when you're doing what you want to do is probably when you'll be doing your best. And pray it is not a hobby so they'll pay you for it.

**Rush Limbaugh**

Seek out that particular mental attribute which makes you feel most deeply and vitally alive, along with which comes the inner voice which says, "This is the real me," and when you have found that attitude, follow it.

**William James**

Let us endeavor to live so that when we come to die even the undertaker will be sorry.

**Mark Twain**

Your work is to discover your work and then with all your heart to give yourself to it.

**Buddha**

What lies behind us and what lies before us are tiny matters, compared to what lies within us.

**Ralph Waldo Emerson**

Great minds have purposes, little minds have wishes.

**Washington Irving**

Happiness comes when we test our skills towards some meaningful purpose.

**John Stosssel**

Strange is our situation here upon earth. Each of us comes for a short visit, not knowing why, yet sometimes seeming to divine a purpose. From the standpoint of daily life, however, there is one thing we do know: that man is here for the sake of other men.

**Albert Einstein**

Every calling is great when greatly pursued.

**Oliver Wendell Holmes**

Desire is the key to motivation, but it's determination and commitment to an unrelenting pursuit of the goal-a commitment to excellence-that will enable you to attain the success you seek.

**Mario Andretti**

The great use of life is to spend if for something that will outlast it.

**Williams James**

Become so wrapped up in something that you forget to be afraid.

**Lady Bird Johnson**

When you discover your mission, you will feel its demand. It will fill you with enthusiasm and a burning desire to get to work on it.

**W. Clement Stone**

The jack of all trades seldom is good at any. Concentrate all of your efforts on one definite chief aim.

**Napoleon Hill**

Use your health, even to the point of wearing it out. That is what it is for. Spend all you have before you die; do not outlive yourself.

**Bernard Shaw**

Joy comes from using your potential.

**Will Schultz**

Love is the master key which opens the gates of happiness.

**Oliver Wendell Holmes**

I look on that man as happy who, when there is question of success, looks into his work for a reply.

**Ralph Waldo Emerson**

The secret of being miserable is to have the leisure to bother about whether you are happy or not. The cure is occupation.

**George Bernard Shaw**

Happiness cannot be traveled to, owned, earned, worn or consumed. Happiness is the spiritual experience of living every minute with love, grace and gratitude.

**Denis Waitley**

Happiness is a Swedish sunset-it is there for all, but most of us look the other way and lose it.

**Mark Twain**

There are as many nights as days, and the one is just as long as the other in the year's course. Even a happy life cannot be without a measure of darkness, and the word 'happy' would lose its meaning if it were not balanced by sadness.

**Carl Jung**

The mere sense of living is joy enough.

**Emily Dickinson**

Happiness is a continuation of happenings which are not resisted.

**Deepak Chopra**

If you want to be happy for a year, plant a garden; If you want to be happy for life, plant a tree.

**English proverb**

Seek not happiness too greedily, and be not fearful of unhappiness.

**Lao Tzu**

---

I'm fulfilled in what I do...I never thought that a lot of money or fine clothes-the finer things of life-would make you happy. My concept of happiness is to be filled in a spiritual sense.

**Coretta Scott King**

Some of us might find happiness if we quit struggling so desperately for it.

**William Feather**

If you want others to be happy, practice compassion. If you want to be happy practice compassion.

**The Dalai Lama**

Those who wish to sing always find a song.

**Swedish proverb**

When one door of happiness closes, another opens.

**Helen Keller**

The way to happiness: keep your heart free from hate, your mind from worry. Live simply, expect little, give much. Fill your life with love. Scatter sunshine. Forget self, think of others. Do as you would be done by. Try this for a week and you will be surprised.

**Norman Vincent Peale**

Self pity is an acid which eats holes in happiness.

**Earl Nightingale**

The big majority of Americans, who are comparatively well off, have developed an ability to have enclaves of people living in the greatest misery without almost noticing them.

**Gunnar Myrdal**

"HAPPINESS"

History is the version of past events that people have decided to agree upon.

**Napoleon**

Bad officials are elected by good citizens who do not vote.

**George Jean Nathan**

Nobody believes the official spokesman... but everybody trusts an unidentified source.

**Ron Nesen**

Lack of will power has caused more failure than lack of intelligence or ability.

**Flower A. Newhouse**

What people say, what people do, and what they say they do are entirely different things.

**Margaret Meade**

The mind is the limit. As long as the mind can envision the fact that you can do something, you can do it-as long as you really believe 100 percent.

**Arnold Schwarzenegger**

Our nettlesome task is to discover how to organize our strength into compelling power.

**Martin Luther King, Jr.**

The quality of a person's life is in direct proportion to their commitment to excellence, regardless of their chosen field of endeavor.

**Vincent Lombardi**

Nobody can be successful unless he loves his work.

**David Sarnoff**

---

The most powerful weapon on earth is the human soul on fire.

**Ferdinand Foch**

I can't imagine a person becoming a success who doesn't give this game of life everything he's got.

**Walter Cronkite**

It takes struggle, a goal and enthusiasm to make a champion.

**Norman Vincent Peale**

Spectacular achievements are always preceded by unspectacular preparation.

**Roger Staubach**

Concentration is the secret of strength in politics, in war, in trade, in short in all management of human affairs.

**Ralph Waldo Emerson**

Anyone can dabble, but once you've made that commitment, your blood has that particular thing in it, and it's very hard for people to stop you.

**Bill Cosby**

Kindness in words creates confidence. Kindness in thinking creates profoundness. Kindness in giving creates love.

**Lao Tzu**

Tenderness and kindness are not signs of weakness and despair but manifestations of strength and resolution.

**Kahlil Gibran**

He has the right to criticize who has the heart to help.

**Abraham Lincoln**

One joy scatters a hundred grief's.

**Chinese Proverb**

Love truth, and pardon error.

**Voltaire**

Life's most urgent question is, what are you doing for others?

**Martin Luther King, Jr.**

It's really a wonder that I haven't dropped all my ideals, because they seem so absurd and impossible to carry out. Yet I keep them, because in spite of everything I still believe that people are really good at heart.

**Anne Frank**

Although the world is very full of suffering, it is also full of the overcoming of it.

**Helen Keller**

Life is an adventure in forgiveness.

**Norman Cousins**

Three things in human life are important. The first is to be kind. The second is to be kind. And the third is to be kind.

**Henry James**

We can let circumstances rule us, or we can take charge and rule our lives from within.

**Earl Nightingale**

Who hath not known ill fortune, never knew himself, or his own virtue.

**Mallett**

Fear is the main source of superstition, and one of the main sources of cruelty. To conquer fear is the beginning of wisdom.

**Bertrand Russell**

Decision is the spark that ignites action. Until a decision is made, nothing happens.... Decision is the courageous facing of issues, knowing that if they are not faced, problems will remain forever unanswered.

**Wilfred A. Peterson**

Always direct your thoughts to those truths that will give you confidence, hope, joy, love, thanksgiving, and turn away your mind from those that inspire you with fear, sadness, depression.

**Bertrand Wilbertforce**

Courage is the first of human qualities because it is the quality which guarantees all others.

**Winston Churchill**

The world isn't interested in the storms you encountered, but whether or not you brought in the ship.

**Raul Armesto**

Any coward can fight a battle when he's sure of winning, but give me a man who has pluck to fight when he's sure of losing.

**George Eliot**

Often the difference between a successful person and a failure is not one has better abilities or ideas, but the courage that one has to bet on one's ideas, to take a calculated risk -- and to act.

**Maxwell Maltz**

You don't develop courage by being happy in your relationships everyday. You develop it by surviving difficult times and challenging adversity.

**Barbara De Angelis**

Every burden is a blessing.

**Robert H. Schuller**

Everyone has talent. What is rare is the courage to follow that talent to the dark place it leads.

**Erica Jong**

Let me not pray to be sheltered from dangers, but to be fearless in facing them. Let me not beg for the stilling of my pain, but for the heart to conquer it.

**Rabindranath Tagore**

It is impossible to win the race unless you venture to run, impossible to win the victory unless you dare to battle.

**Richard DeVos**

It was a high counsel that I once heard given to a young person, "Always do what you are afraid to do."

**Ralph Waldo Emerson**

Obstacles are like wild animals. They are cowards but they will bluff you if they can. If they see you are afraid of them, they are liable to spring upon you; but if you look them squarely in the eye, they will slink out of sight.

**Orison Swett Marden**

The courage of life is often a less dramatic spectacle than the courage of a final moment; but it is no less a magnificent mixture of triumph and tragedy.

**John F. Kennedy**

The battle is not to the strong alone; it is to the vigilant, the active, the brave.

**Patrick Henry**

Whether you be man or woman you will never do anything in this world without courage. It is the greatest quality of the mind next to honor.

**James Allen**

For man's greatest actions are performed in minor struggles. Life, misfortune, isolation, abandonment and poverty are battlefields which have their heroes - obscure heroes who are at times greater than illustrious heroes.

**Victor Hugo**

# *Chapter 6*

The greatest test of courage on earth is to bear defeat without losing heart.

**Robert Green Ingersoll**

Courage is grace under pressure.

**Ernest Hemingway**

It is easy to be brave from a safe distance.

**Aesop**

You can measure a man by the opposition it takes to discourage him.

**Robert C. Savage**

What would life be if we had no courage to attempt anything?

**Vincent Van Gogh**

It often requires more courage to dare to do right than to fear to do wrong.

**Abraham Lincoln**

Stand upright, speak thy thoughts, declare the truth thou hast, that all may share; be bold, proclaim it everywhere. They only live who dare.

**Voltaire**

There are two kinds of adventurers; those who go truly hoping to find adventure and those who go secretly hoping they won't.

**Rabindranath Tagore**

Courage is contagious. When a brave man takes a stand, the spines of others are stiffened.

**Billy Graham**

No bird soars too high, if he soars with his own wings.

**William Blake**

Courage and resolution are the spirit and soul of virtue.

**Thomas Fuller**

I love the man that can smile in trouble, that can gather strength from distress, and grow brave by reflection.

**Thomas Paine**

The battle, sir, is not to the strong alone; it is to the vigilant, the active, the brave.

**Patrick Henry**

Courage is not the absence of fear, but rather the judgment that something else is more important than fear.

**Ambrose Redmoon**

We are living in a world today where lemonade is made from artificial flavors and furniture polish is made from real lemons...

**Alfred E. Newman**

Is not life a hundred times too short for us to bore ourselves?

**Friedrich Nietzsche**

A ship is always referred to as "she" because it costs so much to keep one in paint and powder.

**Chester Nimitz**

When the president does it, that means it is not illegal.

**Richard Nixon**

Laws were made to be broken.

**Christopher North**

Shallow men believe in luck, believe in circumstances -- it was somebody's name, or he happened to be there at the time, or it was so then, and another day would have been otherwise. Strong men believe in cause and effect.

**Ralph Waldo Emerson (1803-1882) American Poet and Essayist**

Excellence is an art won by training and habituation. We do not act rightly because we have virtue or excellence, but rather we have those because we have acted rightly. We are what we repeatedly do. Excellence, then, is not an act but a habit.

**Aristotle**

The world of achievement has always belonged to the optimist.

**J. Harold Wilkins**

It is better to say, "This one thing I do" than to say, "These forty things I dabble in."

**Washington Gladden**

We want to live in the present and the only history that is worth a tinker's damn is the history we make today.

**Henry Ford**

Faith that the thing can be done is essential to any great achievement.

**Thomas N. Carruther**

When we tire of well-worn ways, we seek for new. This restless craving in the souls of men spurs them to climb, and to seek the mountain view.

**Ella Wheeler Wilcox**

The three great essentials to achieving anything worthwhile are; first, hard work, second, stick-to-it-iveness, and third, common sense.

**Thomas A. Edison (1847-1931)**

I wrote this book for a sense of personal satisfaction. Just like taking a good photograph or painting a picture or playing a good golf game or something, it's the thing in itself that justifies it.

**William H. Rehnquist, (1924-)**
**American Supreme Court Chief Justice**

Do better if possible, which always is possible.

**Motto of Francois Constantin,**
**co-founder of watchmaker Vacheron and Constantin.**

Better to do something imperfectly than to do nothing flawlessly.

**Robert Schuller (1926-) American Minister, Evangelist**

Real heroes are men who fall and fail and are flawed, but win out in the end because they've stayed true to their ideals and beliefs and commitments.

**Kevin Costner (1955-) American Actor, Producer and Director**

If I have any message from this then it is if you really have a dream and you want to achieve it then you can and it really is possible.

**Elen Macarthur, quoted after breaking all single-handed woman's**
**records and finishing second in round the world yacht race.**
**February 11th, 2001.**

He was serving his art and his God in the way that his genius - not society or any other authority - dictated.

**Paul Johnson, writing about the artist Donatello**

You, enlightened, self-sufficient, self-governed, endowed with gifts above your fellows, the world expects you to produce as well as to consume, to add to and not to subtract from its store of good, to build up and not to tear down, to ennoble and not degrade.... The time is short, the opportunity is great; therefore, crowd the hours with the best that is in you.

**John Hibben, president of Princeton University,**
**1913 graduation address**

There is in every true woman's heart a spark of heavenly fire, which lies dormant in the broad daylight of prosperity; but which kindles up, and beams and blazes in the dark hour of adversity.

**Washington Irving (1783-1859) American Writer**

My centre is giving way, my right is in retreat; situation excellent. I shall attack.

**Marshall Ferdinand Foch (1851-1929)**
**Supreme Commander of Allied Forces in 1918**

We've all got to go to school, I expect, and we don't all get the same lesson to learn, but the one we do get is our'n, 'taint nobody else's, and if it's real hard, why, it shows the teacher thinks we're capable.

**Rose Terry Cooke**

The one resolution, which was in my mind long before it took the form of a resolution, is the key-note of my life. It is this, always to regard as mere impertinences of fate the handicaps which were placed upon my life almost at the beginning. I resolved that they should not crush or dwarf my soul, but rather be made to blossom, like Aaron's rod, with flowers.

**Helen Keller (1880-1968) American Writer**

The gem cannot be polished without friction, nor man perfected without trials.

**Chinese proverb**

Reduce your plan to writing. The moment you complete this, you will have definitely given concrete form to the intangible desire.

**Napolean Hill**

Adversity is the trial of principle. Without it, a man hardly knows whether he is honest or not.

**Henry Fielding (1707-1754) British Playwright and Novelist**

The abundant life does not come to those who have had a lot of obstacles removed from their path by others. It develops from within and is rooted in strong mental and moral fiber.

**William Mather Lewis**

The beauty of the soul shines out when a man bears with composure one heavy mischance after another, not because he does not feel them, but because he is a man of high and heroic temper.

**Aristotle**

One day in retrospect the years of struggle will strike you as the most beautiful.

**Sigmund Freud**

The effect of great and inevitable misfortune is to elevate those souls which it does not deprive of all virtue.

**Elisabeth Guizot**

Who hath not known ill fortune, never knew himself, or his own virtue.

**Mallett**

Nothing splendid has ever been achieved except by those who dared believe that something inside them was superior to circumstances.

**Bruce Fairchild Barton (1886-1967)**
**American Advertising Executive**

I love the man that can smile in trouble, that can gather strength from distress, and grow brave by reflection.

**Thomas Paine (1737-1809) British-American Writer**

The joy in life is to be used for a purpose. I want to be used up when I die.

**George Bernard Shaw**

One joy scatters a hundred grieves.

**George Bernard Shaw**

Joy is a net of love by which you can catch souls. A joyful heart is the inevitable result of a heart burning with love.

**Mother Teresa**

Live and work but do not forget to play, to have fun in life and really enjoy it.

**Eileen Caddy**

Those who bring sunshine into the lives of others, cannot keep it from themselves.

**Sir James M. Barrie**

Never let anyone steal your joy.

**Mike Richards**

It is only possible to live happily ever after on a day to day basis.

**Margaret Bonnano**

I think I began learning long ago that those who are happiest are those who do the most for others.

**Booker T. Washington**

A happy life must be to a great extent a quiet life, for it is only in an atmosphere of quiet that true joy can live.

**Bertrand Russell**

Real joy comes not from ease or riches or from the praise of men, but from doing something worthwhile.

**Pierre Coneille**

True happiness involves the full use of one's power and talents.

**John W. Gardner**

Joy is not in things, it is in us.

**Richard Wagner**

The art of being happy lies in the power of extracting happiness from common things.

**Henry Ward Beecher**

For every minute you are angry you lose sixty seconds of happiness.

**Ralph Waldo Emerson**

Such is human psychology that if we don't express our joy, we soon cease to feel it.

**Lin Yutang**

You can accomplish by kindness what you cannot by force.

**Publilius Syrus**

Constant kindness can accomplish much. As the sun makes ice melt, kindness causes misunderstanding, mistrust, and hostility to evaporate.

**Albert Schweitzer**

Kind words do not cost much. Yet they accomplish much.

**Blaise Pascal**

There is no beautifier of complexion, or form, or behavior, like the wish to scatter joy and not pain around us.

**Ralph Waldo Emerson**

Let no one ever come to you without leaving better and happier. Be the living expression of God's kindness: kindness in your face, kindness in your eyes, kindness in your smile.

**Mother Teresa**

A kind heart is a fountain of gladness, making everything in its vicinity freshen into smiles.

**Washington Irving**

Kindness is the golden chain by which society is bound together.

**Johann Wolfgang Von Goethe**

No act of kindness, no matter how small, is ever wasted.

**Aesop**

Man is a goal seeking animal. His life only has meaning if he is reaching out and striving for his goals.

**Aristotle**

You've got to get to the stage in life where going for it is more important than winning or losing.

**Arthur Ashe**

In life, the first thing you must do is decide what you really want. Weigh the costs and the results. Are the results worthy of the costs? Then make up your mind completely and go after your goal with all your might.

**Alfred A. Montapert**

There is no such thing in anyone's life as an unimportant day.

**Alexander Woollcott**

A great secret of success is to go through life as a man who never gets used up.

**Albert Schweitzer**

Oh while I live, to be the ruler of life, not a slave, to meet life as a powerful conqueror, and nothing exterior to me will ever take command of me.

**Walt Whitman**

Life is like a dogsled team. If you ain't the lead dog, the scenery never changes.

**Lewis Grizzard**

Life affords no higher pleasure than that of surmounting difficulties, passing from one step of success to another, forming new wishes and seeing them gratified.

**Samuel Johnson**

How do you go from where you are to where you want to be? I think you have to have an enthusiasm for life. You have to have a dream, a goal and you have to be willing to work for it.

**Jim Valvano**

Trust yourself. Create the kind of self that you will be happy to live with all your life. Make the most of yourself by fanning the tiny, inner sparks of possibility into flames of achievement.

**Foster C. McClellan**

The great awareness comes slowly, piece by piece. The path of spiritual growth is a path of lifelong learning. The experience of spiritual power is basically a joyful one.

**M. Scott Peck**

Too often we underestimate the power of a touch, a smile, a kind word, a listening ear, an honest compliment, or the smallest act of caring, all of which have the potential to turn a life around.

**Leo Buscaglia**

The harder the conflict, the more glorious the triumph.

**Thomas Paine**

Adversity is the foundation of virtue.

**Japanese proverb**

Adversity brings knowledge, and knowledge wisdom.

**Welsh Proverb**

A dose of adversity is often as needful as a dose of medicine.

**American Proverb**

All adverse and depressing influences can be overcome, not by fighting, by rising above them.

**Charles Caleb Colton**

Kites rise against, not with the wind. No man has ever worked his passage anywhere in a dead calm.

**John Neal**

A difficult time can be more readily endured if we retain the conviction that our existence holds a purpose - a cause to pursue, a person to love, a goal to achieve.

**John Maxwell**

Obstacles cannot crush me. Every obstacle yields to stern resolve. He who is fixed to a star does not change his mind.

**Leonardo DaVinci**

Patience and perseverance have a magical effect before which difficulties disappear and obstacles vanish.

**John Quincy Adams**

Others can stop you temporarily -- you are the only one who can do it permanently.

**Zig Ziglar**

Depression loses its power when fresh vision pierces the darkness.

**Peter Sinclair**

One's best success comes after their greatest disappointments.

**Henry Ward Beecher**

That which is bitter to endure may be sweet to remember.

**Thomas Fuller**

A man should never be ashamed to own he has been wrong, which is but saying, in other words, that he is wiser today than he was yesterday.

**Alexander Pope**

When you are offended at any man's fault, turn to yourself and study your own failings. Then you will forget your anger.

**Epictetus**

Adversity is the trial of principle. Without it, a man hardly knows whether he is honest or not.

**Henry Fielding**

The one resolution, which was in my mind long before it took the form of a resolution, is the key-note of my life. It is this, always to regard as mere impertinences of fate the handicaps which were placed upon my life almost at the beginning. I resolved that they should not crush or dwarf my soul, but rather be made to blossom, like Aaron's rod, with flowers.

**Helen Keller**

Luck to me is something else. Hard work - and realizing what is opportunity and what isn't.

**Lucille Ball**

Reflect on your present blessings, of which every man has many, not on your past misfortunes, of which all men have some.

**Charles Dickens**

Obstacles don't have to stop you. If you run into a wall, don't turn around and give up. Figure out how to climb it, go through it, or work around it.

**Michael Jordan**

If there were no problems, most of us would be unemployed.

**Zig Ziglar**

Courage and perseverance have a magical talisman, before which difficulties disappear and obstacles vanish into air.

**John Quincy Adams**

Vitality shows in not only the ability to persist but the ability to start over.

**F. Scott Fitzgerald**

Courage doesn't always roar. Sometimes courage is the little voice at the end of the day that says I'll try again tomorrow.

**Mary Annne Radmacher**

Victory is always possible for the person who refuses to stop fighting.

**Napoleon Hill**

It may sound strange, but many champions are made champions by setbacks.

**Bob Richards**

Great men rejoice in adversity, just as brave soldiers triumph in war.

**Seneca**

Prosperity is not without many fears and disasters; and adversity is not without comforts and hopes.

**Francis Bacon**

Self pity is our worst enemy and if we yield to it, we can never do anything wise in the world.

**Helen Keller**

In times like these it is good to remember that there have always been times like these.

**Paul Harvey**

The greatest glory in living lies not in never failing, but in rising every time we fail.

**Nelson Mandella**

Problems are not stop signs, they are guidelines.

**Robert Schuller**

The greatest thing in life is to keep your mind young.

**Henry Ford**

View life as a continuous learning experience.

**Denis Waitley**

You can learn new things at any time in your life if you're willing to be a beginner. If you actually learn to like being a beginner, the whole world opens up to you.

**Barbara Sher**

When men and women are able to respect and accept their differences then love has a chance to blossom.

**John Gray**

Love and you shall be loved.

**Ralph Waldo Emerson**

Tolerance and celebration of individual differences is the fire that fuels lasting love.

**Tom Hannah**

Love does not consist in gazing at each other, but in looking together in the same direction.

**Antoine de Saint-Exupery**

Love is not blind - it sees more, not less. But because it sees more, it is willing to see less

**Rabbi Julius Gordon**

Love looks not with the eyes but with the mind; and therefore is winged Cupid painted blind.

**William Shakespeare**

We are all born for love. It is the principle of existence, and its only end.

**Benjamin Disraeli**

Think lovingly, speak lovingly, act lovingly, and every need shall be supplied.

**James Allen**

We are shaped and fashioned by what we love.

**Johann Wolfgang von Goethe**

Love gives itself; it is not bought.

**Henry Wadsworth Longfellow**

The love we give away is the only love we keep.

**Elbert Hubbard**

Treasure the love you receive above all. It will survive long after your gold and good health have vanished.

**Og Mandingo**

Love is a canvas furnished by nature and embroidered by imagination.

**Voltaire**

---

What we have once enjoyed we can never lose. All that we love deeply becomes a part of us.

**Helen Keller**

Love cures people - both the ones who give it and the ones who receive it.

**Dr. Karl Menninger**

You will find, as you look back upon your life, that the moments when you really lived are the moments when you have done things in the spirit of love.

**Henry Drummond**

Of all earthly music, that which reaches farthest into heaven is the beating of a truly loving heart.

**Henry Ward Beecher**

By the accident of fortune a man may rule the world for a time, but by virtue of love and kindness he may rule the world forever.

**Lao-Tze**

Love is not getting, but giving.

**Henry Van Dyke**

If you love somebody, let them go, for if they return, they were always yours. And if they don't, they never were.

**Kahlil Gibran**

Love is something eternal; the aspect may change, but not the essence.

**Vincent Van Gogh**

One word frees us of all the weight and pain of life; That word is love.

**Sophocles**

To fear love is to fear life, and those who fear life are already three parts dead.

**Bertrand Russell**

Grief and tragedy and hatred are only for a time. Goodness, remembrance and love have no end.

**George Bush**

If you would be loved, love, and be loveable.

**Benjamin Franklin**

Love is the beauty of the soul.

**St. Augustine**

The best proof of love is trust.

**Joyce Brothers**

# *Chapter 7*

At the touch of love, everyone becomes a poet.

**Plato**

Relish love in our old age! Aged love is like aged wine; it becomes more satisfying, more refreshing, more valuable, more appreciated and more intoxicating!

**Leo Buscaglia**

Just don't give up trying to do what you really want to do. Where there is love and inspiration, I don't think you can go wrong.

**Ella Fitzgerald**

Whatever is flexible and living will tend to grow; whatever is rigid and blocked will wither and die.

**Lao Tzu**

The greatest happiness of life is the conviction that we are loved-loved for ourselves, or rather, loved in spite of ourselves.

**Victor Hugo**

Shallow men believe in luck. Strong men believe in cause and effect.

**Ralph Waldo Emerson**

The only thing that overcomes hard luck is hard work.

**Harry Golden**

All of us have bad luck and good luck. The man who persists through the bad luck - who keeps right on going - is the man who is there when the good luck comes - and is ready to receive it.

**Robert Collier**

When I work fourteen hours a day, seven days a week, I get lucky.

**Dr. Armand Hammer**

Luck is a dividend of sweat. The more you sweat, the luckier you get.

**Ray Kroc**

I've found that luck is quite predictable. If you want more luck, take more chances. Be more active. Show up more often.

**Brian Tracy**

When I thought I couldn't go on, I forced myself to keep going. My success is based on persistence, not luck.

**Norman Lear**

It's hard to detect good luck - it looks so much like something you've earned.

**Frank A. Clark**

Depend on the rabbit's foot if you will, but remember it didn't work for the rabbit.

**R.E. Shay**

The golden opportunity you are seeking is in yourself. It is not in your environment; it is not in luck or chance, or the help of others; it is in yourself alone.

**Orison Swett Marsden**

Fortune brings in some boats that are not steered.

**William Shakespeare**

It's not what you've got, it's what you use that makes a difference.

**Zig Ziglar**

I will act as if what I do makes a difference.

**William James**

There is little difference in people, but that little difference makes a big difference. That little difference is attitude. The big difference is whether it is positive or negative.

**W. Clement Stone**

It's easy to make a buck. It's a lot tougher to make a difference.

**Tom Brokaw**

Two roads diverge in a wood, and I took the one less traveled by, and that has made all the difference.

**Robert Frost**

Often the difference between a successful person and a failure is not one has better abilities or ideas, but the courage that one has to bet on one's ideas, to take a calculated risk - and to act.

**Maxwell Maltz**

We must not, in trying to think about how we can make a big difference, ignore the small daily differences we can make which, over time, add up to big differences that we often cannot foresee.

**Marian Wright Edelman**

There are only about a half dozen things that make 80% of the difference in any area of our lives.

**Jim Rohn**

It's not the will to win, but the will to prepare to win that makes the difference.

**Paul "Bear" Bryant**

It's your unlimited power to care and to love that can make the biggest difference in the quality of your life.

**Anthony Robbins**

We all have ability. The difference is how we use it.

**Stevie Wonder**

What we actually learn, from any given set of circumstances, determines whether we become increasingly powerless or more powerful.

**Blaine Lee**

Let us develop the resources of our land, call forth its powers, build up its institutions, promote all its great interests, and see whether we also, in our day and generation, may not perform something worthy to be remembered.

**Blaine Lee**

Ultimately, the only power to which man should aspire is that which he exercises over himself.

**Elie Wiesel**

Real, constructive mental power lies in the creative thought that shapes your destiny, and your hour-by-hour mental conduct produces power for change in your life. Develop a train of thought on which to ride. The nobility of your life as well as your happiness depends upon the direction in which that train of thought is going.

**Laurence J. Peter**

Knowledge is power.

**Francis Bacon**

Knowing others is intelligence; knowing yourself is true wisdom. Mastering others is strength; mastering yourself is true power.

**Lao-Tzu**

No problem can stand the assault of sustained thinking.

**Francois Marie Arouet de Voltaire**

Applaud us when we run, console us when we fall, cheer us when we recover.

**Edmund Burke**

A pat on the back is only a few vertebrae removed from a kick in the pants, but is miles ahead in results.

**Ella Wheeler Wilcox**

Get someone else to blow your horn and the sound will carry twice as far.

**Will Rogers**

Everyone has an invisible sign hanging from their neck saying, "Make me feel important." Never forget this message when working with people.

**Mary Kay**

I can live for two months on a good compliment.

**Mark Twain**

The time to repair the roof is when the sun is shining.

**John F. Kennedy**

Talent alone won't make you a success. Neither will being in the right place at the right time, unless you are ready. The most important question is: "Are your ready?"

**Johnny Carson**

If I had six hours to chop down a tree, I'd spend the first hour sharpening the ax.

**Abraham Lincoln**

Success depends upon previous preparation, and without such preparation there is sure to be failure.

**Confucius**

The values learned on the playing field - how to set goals, endure, take criticism and risks, become team players, use our beliefs, stay healthy and deal with stress - prepare us for life.

**Donna de Varona**

You shouldn't save a pitcher for tomorrow.

**Leo Durocher**

If it is worth playing, it is worth paying the price to win.

**Bear Bryant**

The most important day ever is TODAY.

**James Allen**

For me, winning isn't something that happens suddenly on the field when the whistle blows and the crowds roar. Winning is something that builds physically and mentally every day that you train and every night that you dream.

**Emmitt Smith**

My sun sets to rise again.

**Robert Browning**

Optimism is the faith that leads to achievement. Nothing can be done without hope and confidence.

**Helen Keller**

A problem well stated is a problem half solved.

**John Dewey**

Don't dwell on what went wrong. Instead, focus on what to do next. Spend your energies on moving forward toward finding the answer.

**Denis Waitley**

Hot heads and cold hearts never solved anything.

**Billy Graham**

It's not that I'm so smart, it's just that I stay with problems longer.

**Albert Einstein**

A man who has committed a mistake and doesn't correct it is committing another mistake.

**Confucius**

When the only tool you own is a hammer, every problem begins to resemble a nail.

**Abraham Maslow**

A high character might be produced, I suppose, by continued prosperity, but it has very seldom been the case. Adversity, however it may appear to be our foe, is our true friend; and, after a little acquaintance with it, we receive it as a precious thing -- the prophecy of a coming joy. It should be no ambition of ours to traverse a path without a thorn or stone.

**Charles H. Spurgeon**

You can really have everything you want, if you go after it, but you will have to want it. The desire for success must be so strong within you that it is the very breath of your life -- your first thought when you awaken in the morning, your last thought when you go to bed at night.

**Charles E. Popplestone**

He who finds diamonds must grapple in mud and mire because diamonds are not found in polished stones. They are made.

**Henry B. Wilson**

If we had no winter, the spring would not be so pleasant: if we did not sometimes taste of adversity, prosperity would not be so welcome.

**Charlotte Bronte**

---

Victory is sweetest when you've known defeat.

**Malcolm Forbes (1919-1990) American Publisher**

Take full account of what excellencies which you possess, and in gratitude remember how you would hanker after them, if you had them not.

**Marcus Aurelius (121-180 AD) Roman Emperor, Philosopher**

I am thankful for small mercies. I compared notes with one of my friends who expects everything of the universe, and is disappointed when anything is less than the best, and I found that I begin at the other extreme, expecting nothing, and am always full of thanks for moderate goods.

**Ralph Waldo Emerson (1803-1882)**
**American Poet and Essayist**

The deepest principle of human nature is the craving to be appreciated.

**William James (1842-1910)**
**American Philosopher and Psychologist**

One joy scatters a hundred grieves.

**George Bernard Shaw**

It is better to light one small candle than to curse the darkness.

**Confucius**

You can't have a better tomorrow if you are thinking about yesterday all the time.

**Charles F. Kettering**

Silence may be golden, but can you think of a better way to entertain someone than to listen to him?

**Brigham Young**

Don't find fault find a remedy.

**Henry Ford**

Every day, in every way, I am getting better and better.

**Emile Coue**

Nothing preaches better than the act.

**Benjamin Franklin**

Sometimes if you want to see a change for the better, you have to take things into your own hands.

**Clint Eastwood**

Building a better you is the first step to building a better America.

**Zig Ziglar**

If you build a better mousetrap, you will catch better mice.

**George Gobel**

Some men go through a forest and see no fire wood.

**English Proverb**

Man is so made that when anything fires his soul, impossibilities vanish.

**Jean De La Fontaine**

The finest steel has to go through the hottest fire.

**Richard M. Nixon**

Fire is the test of gold; adversity, of strong men.

**Seneca**

Contentment consists not in adding more fuel, but in taking away some fire.

**Thomas Fuller**

If you aren't fired up with enthusiasm, you'll be fired with enthusiasm.

**Vincent Lombardi**

Be willing to make decisions. That's the most important quality in a good leader. Don't fall victim to what I call the Ready-Aim-Aim-Aim Syndrome. You must be willing to fire.

**T. Boone Pickens**

Success is not the result of spontaneous combustion, you must set yourself on fire first.

**Reggie Leach**

I set myself on fire and people come to watch me burn.

**John Wesley**

In everyone's life, at some time, our inner fire goes out. It is then burst into flame by an encounter with another human being. We should all be thankful for those people who rekindle the inner spirit.

**Albert Schweitzer**

Man is so made that when anything fires his soul, impossibilities vanish.

**Jean De La Fontaine**

Each one of us has a fire in our heart for something. It's our goal in life to find it and to keep it lit.

**Mary Lou Retton**

The starting point of all achievement is desire. Keep this constantly in mind. Weak desires bring weak results, just as a small amount of fire makes a small amount of heat.

**Napoleon Hill**

Through our great good fortune, in our youth our hearts were touched with fire. It was given to us to learn at the outset that life is a profound and passionate thing.

**Oliver Wendell Holmes**

The mind is not a vessel to be filled but a fire to be kindled.

**Plutarch**

If you want to gather honey, don't kick over the beehive.

**Dale Carnegie**

The person who sends out positive thoughts activates the world around him positively and draws back to himself positive results.

**Norman Vincent Peale**

People who produce good results feel good about themselves.

**Ken Blanchard**

Work joyfully and peacefully, knowing that right thoughts and right efforts will inevitably bring about right results.

**James Allen**

Waiting is a trap. There will always be reasons to wait. The truth is, there are only two things in life, reasons and results, and reasons simply don't count.

**Dr. Robert Anthony**

The results you achieve will be in direct proportion to the effort you apply.

**Denis Waitley**

Do not despise the bottom rungs in the ascent to greatness.

**Publilius Syrus**

153

He has half the deed done who has made a beginning.

**Horace**

The beginning is the most important part of the work.

**Plato**

The way to get started is to quit talking and begin doing.

**Walt Disney**

The secret of getting ahead is getting started.

**Sally Berger**

Stop talking. Start walking.

**L.M. Heroux**

We cannot do everything at once, but we can do something at once.

**Calvin Coolidge**

Ideas won't keep; something must be done about them.

**Alfred North Whitehead**

Start by doing what's necessary; then do what's possible; and suddenly you are doing the impossible.

**St. Francis of Assisi**

When there is a start to be made, don't step over! Start where you are.

**Edgar Cayce**

Small opportunities are often the beginning of great enterprises.

**Demosthenes**

Though no one can go back and make a brand new start, anyone can start from now and make a brand new ending.

**Carl Bard**

---

The distance is nothing; it's only the first step that is difficult.

**Marquise du Deffand**

Any man who selects a goal in life which can be fully achieved has already defined his own limitations.

**Cavett Robert**

Far away there in the sunshine are my highest aspirations. I may not reach them, but I can look up and see their beauty, believe in them, and try to follow where they lead.

**Louisa May Alcott**

The most important key to achieving great success is to decide upon your goal and launch, get started, take action, move.

**Brian Tracy**

Aim for the highest.

**Andrew Carnegie**

No matter how carefully you plan your goals they will never be more than pipe dreams unless you pursue them with gusto.

**W. Clement Stone**

Many people fail in life, not for lack of ability or brains or even courage but simply

because they have never organized their energies around a goal.

**Elbert Hubbard**

Some men give up their designs when they have almost reached the goal; while others, on the contrary, obtain a victory by exerting, at the last moment, more vigorous efforts than ever before.

**Herodotus**

When a man does not know what harbor he is making for, no wind is the right wind.

**Lucius Annaeus Seneca**

See things as you would have them be instead of as they are.

**Robert Collier**

All who have accomplished great things have had a great aim, have fixed their gaze on a goal which was high, one which sometimes seemed impossible.

**Orison Swett Marden**

Act like you expect to get into the end zone.

**Joe Paterno**

Your goals are the road maps that guide you and show you what is possible for your life.

**Les Brown**

This one step - choosing a goal and sticking to it - changes everything. Scott Reed Goals. There's not telling what you can do when you get inspired by them. There's no telling what you can do when you believe in them. There's no telling what will happen when you act upon them.

**Jim Rohn**

Difficulties increase the nearer we approach the goal.

**Johann Wolfgang von Goethe**

My philosophy of life is that if we make up our mind what we are going to make of our lives, then work hard toward that goal, we never lose - somehow we win out.

**Ronald Reagan**

People are trapped in history, and history is trapped in them.

**James Baldwin**

History will be kind to me for I intend to write it.

**Winston Churchill**

Make the most of yourself for that is all there is of you.

**Ralph Waldo Emerson**

No harm's done to history by making it something someone would want to read.

**David McCullough**

Live out of your imagination, not your history.

**Stephen R. Covey**

The course of human history is determined, not by what happens in the skies, but by what takes place in our hearts.

**Sir Arthur Kent**

It is a lesson which all history teaches wise men, to put trust in ideas, and not in circumstances.

**Ralph Waldo Emerson**

The history of the world is full of men who rose to leadership, by sheer force of self-confidence, bravery and tenacity.

**Mahatma Gandhi**

Let us resolve to be masters, not the victims, of our history, controlling our own destiny without giving way to blind suspicions and emotions.

**John F. Kennedy**

To me every hour of the light and dark is a miracle. Every cubic inch of space is a miracle.

**Walt Whitman**

The miracle is not to fly in the air, or to walk on the water; but to walk on the earth.

**Chinese Proverb**

Impossible situations can become possible miracles.

**Robert H. Schuller**

Miracles, in the sense of phenomena we cannot explain, surround us on every hand: life itself is the miracle of miracles.

**George Bernard Shaw**

I have found in life that if you want a miracle you first need to do whatever it is you can do - if that's to plant, then plant; if it is to read, then read; if it is to change, then change; if it is to study, then study; if it is to work, then work; whatever you have to do. And then you will be well on your way of doing the labor that works miracles.

**Jim Rohn**

There are no miracles for those that have no faith in them.

**French Proverb**

For the truly faithful, no miracle is necessary. For those who doubt, no miracle is sufficient.

**Nancy Gibbs**

A am realistic - I expect miracles.

**Wayne Dyer**

Where there is great love there are always miracles.

**Willa Cather**

In order to be realist you must believe in miracles.

**David Ben-Gurion**

---

Big goals get big results. No goals gets no results or somebody else's results.

**Mark Victor Hansen**

The secret to productive goal setting is in establishing clearly defined goals, writing them down and then focusing on them several times a day with words, pictures and emotions as if we've already achieved them.

**Denis Waitley**

You, too, can determine what you want. You can decide on your major objectives, targets, aims and destination.

**W. Clement Stone**

Goals give you more than a reason to get up in the morning; they are an incentive to keep you going all day. Goals tend to tap the deeper resources and draw the best out of life.

**Harvey Mackay**

Only those who will risk going too far can possibly find out how far one can go.

**T.S. Eliot**

I do not try to dance better than anyone else. I only try to dance better than myself.

**Mikhail Baryshnikov**

All successful people have a goal. No one can get anywhere unless he knows where he wants to go and what he wants to be or do.

**Norman Vincent Peale**

Remember, what you get by reaching your destination isn't nearly as important as what you become by reaching your goals -- what you will become is the winner you were born to be!

**Zig Ziglar**

We aim above the mark to hit the mark.

**Ralph Waldo Emerson**

I am looking for a lot of men who have an infinite capacity to not know what can't be done.

**Henry Ford**

Don't measure yourself by what you have accomplished, but by what you should have accomplished with your ability.

**John Wooden**

Man is a goal seeking animal. His life only has meaning if he is reaching out and striving for his goals.

**Seneca**

You are never too old to set another goal or to dream a new dream.

**Les Brown**

Goals are dreams we convert to plans and take action to fulfill.

**Zig Ziglar**

Arriving at one goal is the starting point to another.

**John Dewey**

A goal is a dream with a deadline.

**Napoleon Hill**

# Chapter 8

Setting a goal is not the main thing. It is deciding how you will go about achieving it and staying with that plan.

**Tom Landry**

Give me a stock clerk with a goal and I'll give you a man who will make history. Give me a man with no goals and I'll give you a stock clerk.

**J.C. Penney**

A wise man will make more opportunities than he finds.

**Francis Bacon**

Do not be afraid of life. Believe that life is worth living, and your belief will help create the fact.

**William James (1842-1910)**
**American Philosopher and Psychologist**

Most of us can, if we choose, make this world either a prison or a palace.

**Lord Avebury**

Nothing will sustain you more potently than the power to recognize in your humdrum routine, as perhaps it may be thought, the true poetry of life.

**Sir William Osler (1849-1919)**
**Canadian Physician**

Optimism is essential to achievement and it is also the foundation of courage and true progress.

**Nicholas Murray Butler**

Give us, O give us, the man who sings at his work! Be his occupation what it may, he is equal to any of those who follow the same pursuit in silent sullenness. He will do more in the same time -- he will do it better, he will persevere longer. One is scarcely sensible of fatigue whilst he marches to music.

**Thomas Carlyle (1795-1881) Scottish Writer**

Goodwill is the mightiest practical force in the universe.

**Charles F. Dole**

We need a renaissance of wonder. We need to renew, in our hearts and in our souls, the deathless dream, the eternal poetry, the perennial sense that life is miracle and magic.

**E. Merrill Root (1895-1973) American Writer**

Most true happiness comes from one's inner life, from the disposition of the mind and soul. Admittedly, a good inner life is hard to achieve, especially in these trying times. It takes reflection and contemplation and self-discipline.

**William L. Shirer (1904-1993)**
**American Journalist and Historian**

Seek out that particular mental attribute which makes you feel most deeply and vitally alive, along with which comes the inner voice which says, "This is the real me," and when you have found that attitude, follow it.

**William James (1842-1910)**
**American Philosopher and Psychologist**

One must have the adventurous daring to accept oneself as a bundle of possibilities and undertake the most interesting game in the world -- making the most of one's best.

**Harry Emerson Fosdick (1878-1969)**
**American Protestant Minister**

The greatest discovery of my generation is that man can alter his life simply by altering his attitude of mind.

**William James (1842-1910)**

Live your life each day as you would climb a mountain. An occasional glance towards the summit keeps the goal in mind, but many beautiful scenes are to be observed from each new vantage point.

**Harold B. Melchart**

I find that it is not the circumstances in which we are placed, but the spirit in which we face them, that constitutes our comfort.

**Elizabeth T. King**

The first wealth is health.

**Ralph Waldo Emerson**

He who has health, has hope. And he who has hope, has everything.

**Arabian Proverb**

Early to bed and early to rise, makes a man healthy, wealthy, and wise.

**Benjamin Franklin**

Time And health are two precious assets that we don't recognize and appreciate until they have been depleted.

**Denis Waitley**

Take care of your body. It's the only place you have to live.

**Jim Rohn**

The higher your energy level, the more efficient your body. The more efficient your body, the better you feel and the more you will use your talent to produce outstanding results.

**Anthony Robbins**

A man too busy to take care of his health is like a mechanic too busy to take care of his tools.

**Spanish Proverb**

You can set yourself up to be sick, or you can choose to stay well.

**Wayne Dyer**

Money is the most envied, but the least enjoyed. Health is the most enjoyed, but the least envied.

**Charles Caleb Colton**

Remember, if you ever need a helping hand, you'll find one at the end of your arm. . . As you grow older you will discover that you have two hands. One for helping yourself, the other for helping others.

**Audrey Hepburn**

None of us has gotten where we are solely by pulling ourselves up from our own bootstraps. We got here because somebody bent down and helped us.

**Thurgood Marshall**

It is one of the most beautiful compensations of this life that no man can sincerely try to help another without helping himself.

**Ralph Waldo Emerson**

Believe, when you are most unhappy, that there is something for you to do in the world. So long as you can sweeten another's pain, life is not in vain.

**Helen Keller**

There is no higher religion than human service. To work for the common good is the greatest creed.

**Woodrow Wilson**

Blessed are those who can give without remembering and take without forgetting.

**Elizabeth Bibesco**

If you haven't any charity in your heart, you have the worst kind of heart trouble.

**Bob Hope**

How wonderful it is that nobody need wait a single moment before starting to improve the world.

**Anne Frank**

You cannot teach a man anything; you can only help him find it within himself.

**Galileo Galilei**

We can help others in the world more by making the most of yourself than in any other way.

**Earl Nightingale**

We can't help everyone, but everyone can help someone.

**Dr. Loretta Scott**

Our prime purpose in this life is to help others. And if you can't help them, at least don't hurt them.

**Dalai Lama**

Successful people are always looking for opportunities to help others. Unsuccessful people are always asking, "What's in it for me?"

**Brian Tracy**

A good objective of leadership is to help those who are doing poorly to do well and to help those who are doing well to do even better.

**Jim Rohn**

Time and money spent in helping men to do more for themselves is far better than mere giving.

**Henry Ford**

There is no such thing as a self-made man. You will reach your goals only with the help of others.

**George Shinn**

Most of the important things in the world have been accomplished by people who have kept on trying when there seemed to be no help at all.

**Dale Carnegie**

He that won't be counseled can't be helped.

**Benjamin Franklin**

No legacy is so rich as honesty.

**William Shakespeare**

Honesty is the first chapter of the book of wisdom.

**Thomas Jefferson**

Truth is incontrovertible, malice may attack it and ignorance may deride it, but, in the end, there it is.

**Sir Winston Churchill**

If you tell the truth you don't have to remember anything.

**Mark Twain**

Prefer a loss to a dishonest gain; the one brings pain at the moment, the other for all time.

**Chilton**

Hope has as many lives as a cat or a king.

**Henry Wadsworth Longfellow**

Hope is the last thing ever lost.

**Italian Proverb**

Our greatest good, and what we least can spare, is hope.

**Abraham Cowley**

Let your imagination release your imprisoned possibilities.

**Robert H. Schuller**

The imagination is never governed, it is always the ruling and divine power.

**John Ruskin**

Everything you can imagine is real.

**Pablo Picasso**

The opportunities of man are limited only by his imagination. But so few have imagination that there are ten thousand fiddlers to one composer.

**Charles F. Kettering**

The soul without imagination is what an observatory would be without a telescope.

**Henry Ward Beecher**

Every really new idea looks crazy at first.

**Abraham H. Maslow**

Imagination will often carry us to worlds that never were. But without it we go nowhere.

**Carl Sagan**

The man who has no imagination has no wings.

**Muhammad Ali**

First comes thought; then organization of that thought, into ideas and plans; then transformation of those plans into reality. The beginning, as you will observe, is in your imagination.

**Napoleon Hill**

Imagination decides everything.

**John Ruskin**

Imagination gallops; judgment merely walks.

**Prove**

Imagination is the beginning of creation. You imagine what you desire; you will what you imagine; and at last you create what you will.

**George Bernard Shaw**

Anything one man can imagine, other men can make real.

**Jules Verne**

A man, as a general rule, owes very little to what he is born with - a man is what he makes of himself.

**Alexander Graham Bell**

Imagination is the eye of the soul.

**Joubert**

There are no days in life so memorable as those which vibrated to some stroke of the imagination.

**Ralph Waldo Emerson**

Ideas are like rabbits. You get a couple, learn how to handle them, and pretty soon you have a dozen.

**John Steinbeck**

Our aspirations are our possibilities.

**Robert Browning**

Think left and think right and think low and think high. Oh, the thinks you can think up if only you try!

**Dr. Seuss**

An idea is salvation by imagination.

**Frank Lloyd Wright**

Imagination rules the world.

**Napoleon**

There is a boundary to men's passions when they act from feelings; but none when they are under the influence of imagination.

**Edmund Burke**

Your imagination, my dear fellow, is worth more than you imagine.

**Louis Aragon**

I am enough of an artist to draw freely upon my imagination. Imagination is more important than knowledge. Knowledge is limited. Imagination encircles the world.

**Albert Einstein**

The great successful men of the world have used their imagination they think ahead and create their mental picture in all its details, filling in here, adding a little there, altering this a bit and that a bit, but steadily building - steadily building.

**Robert Collier**

Imagination is not a talent of some men but is the health of every man.

**Ralph Waldo Emerson**

To imagine the unimaginable is the highest use of the imagination.

**Cynthia Ozick**

An idea, to be suggestive, must come to the individual with the force of revelation.

**William James**

I am certain of nothing but the holiness of the heart's affections and the truth of imagination.

**John Keats**

The possible's slow fuse is lit by the imagination.

**Emily Dickinson**

Imagination grows by exercise, and contrary to common belief, is more powerful in the mature than in the young.

**W. Somerset Maugham**

I am imagination. I can see what the eyes cannot see. I can hear what the ears cannot hear. I can feel what the heart cannot feel.

**Peter Nivio Zarlenga**

One of the virtues of being very young is that you don't let the facts get in the way of your imagination.

**Sam Levenson**

The human race is governed by its imagination.

**Napoleon Bonaparte**

The quality of the imagination is to flow and not to freeze.

**Ralph Waldo Emerson**

Knowledge is a polite word for dead but not buried imagination.

**E. E. Cummings**

Logics will get you from A to B, imagination will take you everywhere.

**Albert Einstein**

Some men have thousands of reasons why they cannot do what they want to, when all they need is one reason why they can.

**Willis Whitney**

If you can imagine it, you can achieve it; if you can dream it, you can become it.

**William Arthur Ward**

Imagination ... its limits are only those of the mind itself.

**Rod Serling**

Age considers; youth ventures.

**Rabindranath Tagore**

What would it be like if you lived each day, each breath, as a work of art in progress? Imagine that you are a masterpiece unfolding, every second of every day, a work of art taking form with every breath.

**Thomas Crum**

Anybody can do anything that he imagines.

**Henry Ford**

The mind of man is capable of anything because everything is in it, all the past as well as the future.

**Joseph Conrad**

Losers visualize the penalties of failure. Winners visualize the rewards of success.

**Dr. Rob Gilbert**

The only way to find the limits of the possible is by going beyond them to the impossible.

**Arthur C. Clarke**

"HAPPINESS"

Imagination is the highest kite one can fly.

**Lauren Bacall**

The idea is in thyself. The impediment, too, is in thyself.

**Thomas Carlyle**

We are governed not by armies and police, but by ideas.

**Mona Caird**

And when you have reached the mountain top, then you shall begin to climb.

**Kahlil Gibran**

Every child is an artist. The problem is how to remain an artist once he grows up.

**Pablo Picasso**

Not everything that can be counted counts, and not everything that counts can be counted.

**Albert Einstein**

The great successful men of the world have used their imagination ... they think ahead and create their mental picture in all its details, filling in here, adding a little there, altering this a bit and that a bit, but steadily building - steadily building.

**Robert Collier**

An idea is salvation by imagination.

**Frank Lloyd Wright**

Every great advance in science has issued from a new audacity of imagination.

**Robert Collier**

What is now proved was once imagined.

**William Blake**


I am certain of nothing but of the holiness of the hearts affection, and the truth of the imagination.

**John Keats**


You can't depend on your eyes when your imagination is out of focus.

**Mark Twain**


To swear off making mistakes is very easy. All you have to do is swear off having ideas.

**Leo Burnett**


A man's mind, once stretched by a new idea, never goes back to its original dimensions.

**Oliver Wendell Holmes**


It's time to start living the life you've imagined.

**Henry James**


The man who will use his skill and constructive imagination to see how much he can give for a dollar instead of how little he can give for a dollar is bound to succeed.

**Henry Ford**


Live out of your imagination, not your history.

**Stephen Covey**


If a man is called to be a street sweeper, he should sweep streets even as Michelangelo painted, or Beethoven composed music, or Shakespeare wrote poetry. He should sweep streets so well that the host of heaven and earth will pause to say, here lived a great street sweeper who did his job well.

**Martin Luther King, Jr.**

Laws control the lesser man. Right conduct controls the greater one.

**Chinese proverb**

Love all, trust a few, do wrong to none.

**William Shakespeare**

It's kind of fun to do the impossible.

**Walt Disney**

I think of life itself now as a wonderful play that I've written for myself... and so my purpose is to have the utmost fun playing my part.

**Shirley MacLaine**

While there is a chance of the world getting through its troubles, I hold that a reasonable man has to behave as though he were sure of it. If at the end your cheerfulness is not justified, at any rate you will have been cheerful.

**H.G. Wells**

The humorous man recognizes that absolute purity, absolute justice, absolute logic and perfection are beyond human achievement and that men have been able to live happily for thousands of years in a state of genial frailty.

**Brooks Atkinson**

Optimism is the faith that leads to achievement. Nothing can be done without hope and confidence.

**Helen Keller (1880-1968) American Writer**

Think positively and masterfully with confidence and faith, and life becomes more secure, more fraught with action, richer in achievement and experience.

**Eddie Rickenbacker (1890-1973)**
**American Aviator and Business Executive**

He is a man of sense who does not grieve for what he has not, but rejoices in what he has.

**Epictetus (55-135 AD) Roman Philosopher**

Would you sell both your eyes for a million dollars...or your two legs..or your hands...or your hearing? Add up what you do have, and you'll find you won't sell them for all the gold in the world. The best things in life are yours, if you can appreciate them.

**Dale Carnegie (1888-1955) American Author and Speaker**

If there is one thing upon this earth that mankind love and admire better than another, it is a brave man, -- it is the man who dares to look the devil in the face and tell him he is a devil.

**James A. Garfield**

What ought one to say then as each hardship comes? I was practicing for this, I was training for this.

**Epictetus (55-135 AD) Roman Philosopher**

Find a purpose in life so big it will challenge every capacity to be at your best.

**David O. McKay (1873-1970)**
**American Religious Leader**

You must do the thing you think you cannot do.

**Eleanor Roosevelt (1884-1962) American First**

If you cannot understand that there is something in a man which responds to the challenge of this mountain and goes out to meet it, that the struggle is the struggle of life itself upward and forever upward, then you won't see why we go. What we get from this adventure is just sheer joy. (reflecting on the challenge of climbing Mount McKinley, the highest peak on the North American continent)

**George Leigh Mallory (1886-1924)**
**English Mountain Climber**

Trials, temptations, disappointments -- all these are helps instead of hindrances, if one uses them rightly. They not only test the fibre of a character, but strengthen it. Every conquered temptation represents a new fund of moral energy. Every trial endured and weathered in the right spirit makes a soul nobler and stronger than it was before.

**James Buckham**

Some day, in years to come, you will be wrestling with the great temptation, or trembling under the great sorrow of your life. But the real struggle is here, now, in these quiet weeks. Now it is being decided whether, in the day of your supreme sorrow or temptation, you shall miserably fail or gloriously conquer. Character cannot be made except by a steady, long continued process.

**Phillips Brooks (1835-1893) American Bishop**

# Chapter 9

What lies behind us and what lies before us are tiny matters compared to what lies within us.

**William Morrow**

The world has battle-room for all. Go fight and conquer if ye can. But if ye rise or if ye fall, Be each, pray God, a gentleman!
**William Makepeace Thackeray (1811-1863) Indian Novelist**

Every man is valued in this world as he shows by his conduct that he wishes to be valued.
**Jean De La Bruyere (1645-1696) French Moralist and Writer**

The principles we live by, in business and in social life, are the most important part of happiness. We need to be careful, upon achieving happiness, not to lose the virtues which have produced it.

**Harry Harrison**

Justice is a certain rectitude of mind whereby a man does what he ought to do in circumstances confronting him.

**St. Thomas Aquinas**

To give real service you must add something which cannot be bought or measured with money, and that is sincerity and integrity.

**Donald A. Adams**

Class is an aura of confidence that is being sure without being cocky. Class has nothing to do with money. Class never runs scared. It is self-discipline and self-knowledge. It's the sure footedness that comes with having proved you can meet life.

**Ann Landers**

Simplicity of character is no hindrance to subtlety of intellect.

**John Morley**

The only guide to man is his conscience; the only shield to his memory is the rectitude and sincerity of his actions. It is very imprudent to walk through life without this shield, because we are so often mocked by the failure of our hopes and the upsetting of our calculations; but with this shield, however the fates may play, we march always in the ranks of honor.

**- Tribute to Neville Chamberlain; 1940 Sir Winston Churchill (1874-1965) British Politician**

Character may be manifested in the great moments, but it is made in the small ones.

**Phillips Brooks (1835-1893) American Bishop**

The self is not something that one finds. It is something that one creates.

**Thomas Szasz (1920-) American Psychiatrist**

In the middle of difficulty lies opportunity.

**Albert Einstein**

You are not called to be a canary in a cage. You are called to be an eagle, and to fly sun to sun, over continents.

**Henry David Thoreau**

I feel that the greatest reward for doing is the opportunity to do more.

**Jonas Salk**

Tomorrow is the most important thing in life. Comes into us at midnight very clean. It's perfect when it arrives and puts itself in our hands. It hopes we've learned something from yesterday.

**John Wayne**

The moment of enlightenment is when a person's dreams of possibilities become images of probabilities.

**Vic Braden**

Failure is the opportunity to begin again, more intelligently.

**Henry Ford**

The first one gets the oyster the second gets the shell.

**Andrew Carnegie**

Employ your time in improving yourself by other men's writings so that you shall come easily by what others have labored hard for.

**Sophocles**

There is a great deal of unmapped country within us which would have to be taken in account in an explanation of our gusts and storms.

**George Eliot**

Fortune knocks but once, but misfortune has much more patience.

**Laurence Peter**

The heights of great men reached and kept, were not obtained by sudden flight, but they, while their companions slept were toiling upward in the night.

**Henry Wadsworth Longfellow**

What happened yesterday is history. What happens tomorrow is a mystery. What we do today makes a difference -- the precious present moment.

**Nick Saban**

When the student is ready, the master appears.

**Buddhist proverb**

Become a possibilitarian. No mater how dark things seem to be or actually are, raise your sights and see possiblities-always see them for they're always there.

**Norman Vincent Peale**

The more you seek security, the less of it you have. But the more you seek opportunity, the more likely it is that you will achieve the security that you desire.

**Brian Tracy**

Obstacles can't stop you. Problems can't stop you. Most of all other people can't stop you. Only you can stop you.

**Jeffrey Gitomer**

Adversity has the effect of eliciting talents, which in prosperous circumstances would have lain dormant.

**Horace**

You may not realize it when it happens, but at kick in the teeth may be the best thing in the world for you.

**Walt Disney**

Too many of us are not living our dreams because we are living our fears.

**Les Brown**

You can conquer almost any fear if you will only make up your mind to do so. For remember, fear doesn't exist anywhere except in the mind.

**Dale Carnegie**

Procrastination is the fear of success. People procrastinate because they are afraid of the success that they know will result if they move ahead now. Because success is heavy, carries a responsibility with it, it is much easier to procrastinate and live on the 'someday I'll' philosophy.

**Denis Waitley**

Of all the liars in the world, sometimes the worst are your own fears.

**Rudyard Kipling**

Nothing can bring you peace but yourself.

**Ralph Waldo Emerson**

The more tranquil a man becomes, the greater is his success, his influence, his power for good. Calmness of mind is one of the beautiful jewels of wisdom.

**James Allen**

Holding on to anger is like grasping a hot coal with the intent of throwing it at someone else; you are the one getting burned.

**Buddha**

Always direct your thoughts to those truths that will give you confidence, hope, joy, love, thanksgiving, and turn away your mind from those that inspire you with fear, sadness, depression.

**Bertrand Wilbertforce**

Watch your manner of speech if you wish to develop a peaceful state of mind. Start each day by affirming peaceful, contented and happy attitudes and your days will tend to be pleasant and successful.

**Norman Vincent Peale**

How beautiful it is to do nothing, and then rest afterward.

**Spanish proverb**

In the midst of movement and chaos keep stillness inside of you.

**Deepak Chopra**

If there is light in the soul, There will be beauty in the person. If there is beauty in the person, There will be harmony in the house. If there is harmony in the house, There will be order in the nation. If there is order in the nation, There will be peace in the world.

**Chinese Proverb**

It is requisite for the relaxation of the mind that we make use, from time to time, of playful deeds and jokes.

**Thomas Aquinas**

When a man finds no peace within himself it is useless to seek it elsewhere.

**L. A. Rouchefoliocauld**

Even a happy life cannot be without a measure of darkness, and the word happy would lose its meaning if it were not balanced by sadness. It is far better to take things as they come along with patience and equanimity.

**Carl Jung**

Be so strong that nothing can disturb your peace of mind.

**Christian Larson**

Talk peaceful to be peaceful.

**Norman Vincent Peale**

When you aim for perfection, you discover it's a moving target.

**Geoffrey F. Fisher**

The pursuit of perfection often impedes improvement.

**George F. Will**

The true perfection of man lies not in what man has, but in what man is.

**Oscar Wilde**

Aim at perfection in everything, though in most things it is unattainable. However, they who aim at it, and persevere, will come much nearer to it than those whose laziness and despondency make them give it up as unattainable.

**Lord Chesterfield**

The harder the conflict, the more glorious the triumph. What we obtain too cheap, we esteem too lightly; it is dearness only that gives everything its value. I love the man that can smile in trouble, that can gather strength from distress and grow brave by reflection. 'Tis the business of little minds to shrink; but he whose heart is firm, and whose conscience approves his conduct, will pursue his principles unto death.

**Thomas Paine**

I do not think that there is any other quality so essential to success of any kind as the quality of perseverance. It overcomes almost everything, even nature.

**John D. Rockefeller**

Your biggest break can come from never quitting. Being at the right place at the right time can only happen when you keep moving toward the next opportunity.

**Arthur Pine**

You've got to say, I think that if I keep working at this and want it badly enough I can have it. It's called perseverance.

**Lee Iacocca**

Perseverance gives power to weakness, and opens to poverty the world's wealth. It spreads fertility over the barren landscape, and buds the choicest flowers and fruits spring up and flourish in the desert abode of thorns and briars.

**Samuel G. Goodrich**

If I had to select one quality, one personal characteristic that I regard as being most highly correlated with success, whatever the field, I would pick the trait of persistence. Determination. The will to endure to the end, to get knocked down seventy times and get up off the floor saying, Here comes number seventy-one!

**Richard M. DeVos**

Man must cease attributing his problems to his environment, and learn again to exercise his will - his personal responsibility.

**Albert Schweitzer**

Accept responsibility for your life. Know that it is you who will get you where you want to go, no one else.

**Les Brown**

A man, as a general rule, owes very little to what he is born with - a man is what he makes of himself.

**Alexander Graham Bell**

The greatest gifts you can give your children are the roots of responsibility and the wings of independence.

**Denis Waitley**

You must take personal responsibility. You cannot change the circumstances, the seasons, or the wind, but you can change yourself. That is something you have charge of.

**Jim Rohn**

I believe that every right implies a responsibility; every opportunity an obligation; every possession, a duty.

**John D. Rockefeller**

Whatever happens, take responsibility.

**Anthony Robbins**

We must reject the idea that every time a law's broken, society is guilty rather than the lawbreaker. It is time to restore the American precept that each individual is accountable for his actions.

**Ronald Reagan**

The best job goes to the person who can get it done without passing the buck or coming back with excuses.

**Napoleon Hill**

Success on any major scale requires you to accept responsibility ... In the final analysis, the one quality that all successful people have ... is the ability to take on responsibility.

**Michael Korda**

Man does not live by words alone, despite the fact that sometimes he has to eat them.

**Broderick Crawford**

Don't spend your precious time asking 'Why isn't the world a better place?' It will only be time wasted. The question to ask is 'How can I make it better?' To that there is an answer.

**Leo F. Buscaglia**

When it's all over, it's not who you were ... it's whether you made a difference.

**Bob Dole**

Put all excuses aside and remember this: YOU are capable.

**Zig Ziglar**

Each player must accept the cards that life deals him or her. But once in hand one must decide how to play the cards in order to win the game.

**Voltaire**

We all have dreams. But in order to make dreams into reality, it takes an awful lot of determination, dedication, self-discipline, and effort.

**Jesse Owens**

Within each of us lies the power of our consent to health and sickness, to riches and poverty, to freedom and to slavery. It is we who control these, and not another.

**Richard Bach**

Life is a gift, and it offers us the privilege, opportunity, and responsibility to give something back by becoming more.

**Anthony Robbins**

Knowing is not enough; we must apply. Willing is not enough; we must do.

**Johann von Goethe**

Hold yourself responsible for a higher standard than anybody else expects of you. Never excuse yourself. Never pity yourself. Be a hard master to yourself - and be lenient to everybody else.

**Henry Ward Beecher**

Take your life in your own hands, and what happens? A terrible thing: no one to blame.

**Erica Jong**

When a man points a finger at someone else, he should remember that four of his fingers are pointing at himself.

**Louis Nizer**

It is a painful thing to look at your own trouble and know that you yourself and no one else has made it.

**Sophocles**

The strongest principle of growth lies in human choice.

**George Eliot**

Do more than is required of you.

**George S. Patton**

Adversity causes some men to break, others to break records.

**William A. Ward**

No pressure, no diamonds.

**Mary Case**

I would never have amounted to anything were it not for adversity. I was forced to come up the hard way.

**J. C. Penney**

If we study the lives of great men and women carefully and unemotionally we find that, invariably, greatness was developed, tested and revealed through the darker periods of their lives. One of the largest tributaries of the RIVER OF GREATNESS is always the STREAM OF ADVERSITY.

**Cavett Robert**

When it gets dark enough you can see the stars.

**Lee Salk**

One who gains strength by overcoming obstacles possesses the only strength which can overcome adversity.

**Albert Schweitzer**

I was not only proud of what he did in the pool, but I was proud of the way he handled himself out of the pool. The measure of a true champion is not how they win. It's how they handle defeat -a quote above is about his son.

**Gary Hall, Sr. (1951-)**
**American Olympic Silver Medalist in Swimming**

The four cornerstones of character on which this nation was built are: Initiative, Imagination, Individuality and Independence.

**Eddie Rickenbacker (1890-1973)**
**American Aviator and Business Executive**

You can easily judge the character of others by how they treat those who can do nothing for them or to them.

**Malcolm Forbes (1919-1990) American Publisher**

Confidence on the outside begins by living with integrity on the inside.

**Brian Tracy**

Nearly all men can stand adversity, but if you want to test a man's character, give him power.

**Abraham Lincoln (1809-1865)**

Thoughtfulness for others, generosity, modesty and self-respect are the qualities which make a real gentleman or lady.

**Thomas Henry Huxley (1825-1895) British Scientist**

I am not bound to win, but I am bound to be true. I am not bound to succeed, but I am bound to live by the light that I have.

**Abraham Lincoln (1809-1865) 16th President of the United States**

Conscience is the root of all true courage; if a man would be brave let him obey his conscience.

**James Freeman Clarke (1810-1888)**
**American Unitarian Minister and Author**

Principle -- particularly moral principle -- can never be a weathervane, spinning around this way and that with the shifting winds of expediency. Moral principle is a compass forever fixed and forever true.

**Edward R. Lyman**

The world stands aside to let anyone pass who knows where he is going.

**David Starr Jordan (1851-1931)**
**American, University President, Author**

Moral courage is a virtue of higher cast and nobler origin than physical. It springs from a consciousness of virtue and renders a man, in the pursuit or defense of right, superior to the fear of reproach, opposition, or contempt.

**Samuel Goodrich**

Purity of soul cannot be lost without consent.

**St. Augustine**

Expedients are for the hour, but principles are for the ages. Just because the rains descend, and the winds blow, we cannot afford to build on shifting sands.

**Henry Ward Beecher (1813-1887)**
**American Presbyterian Minister**

The reason most people never reach their goals is that they don't define them, learn about them or even seriously consider them as believable or achievable. Winners can tell you where they are going, what they plan to do along the way, and who will be sharing the adventure with them.

**Denis Waitley**

The height of your accomplishments will equal the depth of your convictions.

**William F. Scolavino**

True religion is the life we lead, not the creed we profess.

**Louis Nizer (1902-1994) American Lawyer**

In matters of style, swim with the current; in matters of principle, stand like a rock.

**Thomas Jefferson (1743-1826)**
**Third President of the United States**

Self-reliance is the only road to true freedom, and being one's own person is its ultimate reward.

**Patricia Sampson**

Freedom is the right to live as we wish.

**Epictetus**

History does not long entrust the care of freedom to the weak or the timid.

**Dwight D. Eisenhower**

I know but one freedom and that is the freedom of the mind.

**Antoine De Saint-Exupery**

Freedom is the last, best hope of earth.

**Abraham Lincoln**

Everything that is really great and inspiring is created by the individual who can labor in freedom.

**Albert Einstein**

In the truest sense, freedom cannot be bestowed; it must be achieved.

**Franklin D. Roosevelt**

---

You cannot be friends upon any other terms than upon the terms of equality.

**Woodrow T. Wilson**

A smile is the light in your window that tells others that there is a caring, sharing person inside.

**Denis Waitley**

Winning has always meant much to me, but winning friends has meant the most.

**Babe Didrikson Zaharias**

It takes a long time to grow an old friend.

**John Leonard**

There is no friend as loyal as a book.

**Ernest Hemingway**

If you think nobody cares if you're alive, try missing a couple of car payments.

**Flip Wilson**

I'm not crazy about reality, but it's still the only place to get a decent meal.

**Groucho Marx**

Older people shouldn't eat health food, they need all the preservatives they can get.

**Robert Orben**

You have to stay in shape. My grandmother, she started walking five miles a day when she was 60. She's 97 today and we don't know where the hell she is.

**Ellen Degeneres**

For fast acting relief try slowing down.

**Lily Tomlin**

About the time we can make ends meet, somebody moves the ends.

**Herbert Hoover**

Catch a man a fish, and you can sell it to him. Teach a man to fish, and you ruin a wonderful business opportunity.

**Karl Marx**

Happiness is having a large, loving, caring, close-knit family in another city.

**George Burns**

Be true to your teeth and they won't be false to you.

**Soupy Sales**

I stopped believing in Santa Claus when I was six. Mother took me to see him in a department store and he asked for my autograph.

**Shirley Temple Black**

Winning is everything. The only ones who remember you when you come second are your wife and your dog.

**Damon Hill**

We owe a lot to Thomas Edison - if it wasn't for him, we'd be watching television by candlelight.

**Milton Berle**

If we could sell our experiences for what they cost us ... we would all be millionaires.

**Abigail Van Buren**

Everyone knows what a hypocrite is…That's the guy who gripes about the sex, violence and nudity on his VCR.

**Zig Ziglar**

Lotto fever hit New York again this week, and like the old saying goes, 'You gotta be in it to win it'… but first, you gotta have a dead end job so pathetic you're willing to kill five hours standing in line for a 1 in 25 million chance.

**Dennis Miller**

There is nothing so annoying as to have two people talking when you're busy interrupting.

**Mark Twain**

Too bad the only people who know how to run the country are busy driving cabs and cutting hair.

**George Burns**

# Chapter 10

Only one man in a thousand is a leader of men -- the other 999 follow women.

**Groucho Marx**

I asked a ref if he could give me a technical foul for thinking bad things about him. He said, of course not. I said, well, I think you stink. And he have me a technical. You can't trust em.

**Jim Valvano**

You can observe a lot by watching.

**Yogi Berra**

Women will never be as successful as men because they have no wives to advise them.

**Dick Van Dyke**

Don't confuse fame with success. Madonna is one; Helen Keller is the other.

**Erma Bombeck**

My success has allowed me to strike out with a higher class of women.

**Woody Allen**

The nice part about being a pessimist is that you are constantly being either proven right or pleasantly surprised.

**George Will**

The Supreme Court has ruled that they cannot have a nativity scene in Washington, D.C. This wasn't for any religious reasons. They couldn't find three wise men and a virgin.

**Jay Leno**

I'm glad I don't play anymore. I could never learn all those handshakes.

**Phil Rizzuto**

A study in the Washington Post says that women have better verbal skills than men. I just have one thing to say to the authors of that study: Duh.

**Conan O'Brien**

Tis the business of little minds to shrink, but he whose heart is firm, and whose conscience approves his conduct, will pursue his principles unto death.

**Thomas Paine (1737-1809) British-American Writer**

It is the soul's duty to be loyal to its own desires.

**Rebecca West**

Happy is he who dares courageously to defend what he loves.

**Ovid (Publius Ovidius Naso) (43-17 BC) Roman Poet**

Two things fill the mind with ever new and increasing wonder and awe, the more often and the more seriously reflection concentrates upon them: the starry heaven above me and the moral law within me.

**Immanuel Kant (1724-1804) German Philosopher**

To be yourself in a world that is constantly trying to make you something else is the greatest accomplishment.

**Ralph Waldo Emerson**

A great deal of talent is lost to the world for want of a little courage. Every day sends to their graves obscure men whose timidity prevented them from making a first effort.

**Sydney Smith**

Bravery is being the only one who knows you're afraid.

**Franklin P Jones**

If we are to survive, we must have ideas, vision, and courage. These things are rarely produced by committees.

**Arthur Schlesinger**

Tell a man he is brave, and you help him to become so.

**Thomas Carlyle**

What counts is not necessarily the size of the dog in the fight - it's the size of the fight in the dog.

**Dwight D. Eisenhower**

Determine what specific goal you want to achieve. Then dedicate yourself to its attainment with unswerving singleness of purpose, the trenchant zeal of a crusader.

**Paul J. Meyer**

Courage is not the absence of fear, but rather the judgment that something else is more important than fear.

**Ambrose Redmoon**

My strength is as the strength of ten, because my heart is pure.

**Alfred Lord Tennyson**

You can stand tall without standing on someone. You can be a victor without having victims.

**Harriet Woods**

Before success comes in any man's life he is sure to meet with much temporary defeat and, perhaps, some failures. When defeat overtakes a man, the easiest and most logical thing to do is to quit. That is exactly what the majority of men do.

**Napoleon Hill**

For all sad words of tongue or pen, The saddest are these: "It might have been."

**John Greenleaf Whittier**

Life is 10 percent what you make it and 90 percent how you take it.

**Irving Berlin**

Anybody can do just about anything with himself that he really wants to and makes up his mind to do. We are all capable of greater things than we realize.

**Norman Vincent Peale**

Good timber does not grow with ease. The stonger the wind the stronger the trees.

**Williard Marriott**

Moral courage is the most valuable and usually the most absent characteristic in men.

**George Patton**

It was courage, faith, endurance and a dogged determination to surmount all obstacles that built this bridge.

**John Watson**

Promise yourself to be so strong that nothing can disturb your peace of mind.

**Christian Larson**

It is what you do about what happens that counts.

**Jim Rohn**

Courage is the price that life exacts for granting peace. The bravest are surely those who have the clearest vision of what is before them, glory and danger alike, and yet notwithstanding, go out and meet it.

**Thucydides**

The characteristic of a genuine heroism is its persistency. All men have wandering impulses, fits and starts of generosity. But when you have resolved to be great, abide by yourself, and do not weakly try to reconcile yourself with the world. The heroic cannot be the common, nor the common the heroic.

**Ralph Waldo Emerson**

A timid person is frightened before a danger, a coward during the time, and a courageous person afterwards.

**Paul Richter**

Any time you try to win everything, you must be willing to lose everything.

**Larry Csonka**

Be bold and courageous. When you look back on your life, you'll regret the things you didn't do more than the ones you did.

**H. Jackson Brown, Jr.**

The human spirit is stronger than anything that can happen to it.

**George S. Patton**

The block of granite, which was an obstacle in the path of the weak, becomes a stepping stone in the path of the strong.

**Thomas Carlyle**

Take chances. When rowing forward, the boat may rock.

**Chinese proverb**

Our greatest glory is not in never failing, but in rising up every time we fail.

**Ralph Waldo Emerson**

Behold the turtle. He only makes progress when he sticks his neck out.

**James Bryant Conant**

Courage is being scared to death...and saddling up anyway.

**John Wayne**

In the beginning of a change, the patriot is a scarce man, and brave, and hated scorned. When his cause succeeds, the timid join him for then it costs nothing to be a patriot.

**Mark Twain**

The time to take counsel of your fears is before you make an important battle decision. That's the time to listen to every fear you can imagine! When you have collected all the facts and fears and made you decision, turn off all your fears and go ahead!

**George S. Patton**

Coward: One who, in a perilous emergency, thinks with his legs.

**Ambrose Bierce**

Courage is resistance to fear, mastery of fear, not absence of fear.

**Mark Twain**

It is well to think well; it is divine to act well.

**Horace Mann**

One way to keep momentum going is to have constantly greater goals.

**Michael Korda**

Sometimes being pushed to the wall gives you the momentum necessary to get over it!

**Peter de Jager**

The most important thing you can do to achieve your goals is to make sure that as soon as you set them, you immediately begin to create momentum.

**Anthony Robbins**

Success requires first expending ten units of effort to produce one unit of results. Your momentum will then produce ten units of results with each unit of effort.

**Charles J. Givens**

A penny saved is a penny earned.

**Benjamin Franklin**

If money is your hope for independence you will never have it. The only real security that a man will have in this world is a reserve of knowledge, experience, and ability.

**Henry Ford**

Make no mistake, my friend, it takes more than money to make men rich.

**A. P. Gouthey**

Before you speak, listen. Before you write, think. Before you spend, earn. Before you invest, investigate. Before you criticize, wait. Before you pray, forgive. Before you quit, try. Before you retire, save. Before you die, give.

**William A. Ward**

Inspirations never go in for long engagements; they demand immediate marriage to action.

**Brendan Francis**

The ones who want to achieve and win championships motivate themselves.

**Mike Ditka**

To be successful, have your heart in your business and your business in your heart.

**Thomas Watson**

Desire creates the power.

**Raymond Hollingwell**

People often say that motivation doesn't last. Well, neither does bathing - that's why we recommend it daily.

**Zig Ziglar**

Motivation is a fire from within. If someone else tries to light that fire under you, chances are it will burn very briefly.

**Stephen Covey**

A strong passion for any object will ensure success, for the desire of the end will point out the means.

**Henry Hazlitt**

Heart in champions has to do with the depth of your motivation and how well your mind and body react to pressure.

**Bill Russell**

Mountains cannot be surmounted except by winding paths.

**Johann Wolfgang von Goethe**

It isn't the mountainhead that wears you out; it's the grain of sand in your shoe.

**Robert W. Service**

Great things are done when men and mountains meet.

**William Blake**

The difference between a mountain and a molehill is your perspective.

**Al Neuharth**

Winners take time to relish their work, knowing that scaling the mountain is what makes the view from the top so exhilarating.

**Denis Waitley**

---

What we play is life.

**Louis Armstrong**

If you look deep enough you will see music; the heart of nature being everywhere music.

**Thomas Carlyle**

Music has charms to soothe the savage beast, to soften rocks or bend a knotted oak.

**William Congreve**

A song will outlive all sermons in the memory.

**Henry Giles**

Music is the movement of sound to reach the soul for the education of its virtue.

**Plato**

If music be the food of love; play on.

**William Shakespeare**

Of all the music that reached farthest into heaven, it is the beating of a loving heart.

**Henry Ward Beecher**

You can discover more about a person in an hour of play than in a year of conversation.

**Plato**

Work consists of whatever a body is obliged to do. Play consists of whatever a body is not obliged to do.

**Mark Twain**

We don't stop playing because we grow old; we grow old because we stop playing.

**George Bernard Shaw**

Few things in the world are more powerful than a positive push. A smile. A word of optimism and hope. A "you can do it" when things are tough.

**Richard M. DeVos**

I have made it a rule of my life never to regret and never to look back. Regret is an appalling waste of energy ... you can't build on it; it's only good for wallowing in.

**Katherine Mansfield**

Little minds attain and are subdued by misfortunes; but great minds rise above them.

**Washington Irving**

Give me a lever long enough and a prop strong enough. I can single-handedly move the world.

**Archimedes**

The future of civilization depends on our overcoming the meaninglessness and hopelessness that characterizes the thoughts of men today.

**Albert Schweitzer**

Aerodynamically, the bumble bee shouldn't be able to fly, but the bumble bee doesn't know it so it goes on flying anyway.

**Mary Kay Ash**

The more you recognize and express gratitude for the things you have, the more you will have to express gratitude for.

**Zig Ziglar**

One of the redeeming things about being an athlete is redefining what is humanly possible.

**Lance Armstrong**

It doesn't matter how many say it cannot be done or how many people have tried it before; it's important to realize that whatever you're doing, it's you first attempt at it.

**Wally Amos**

The young do not know enough to be prudent, and therefore they attempt the impossible, and achieve it, generation after generation.

**Pearl Buck**

I am always doing things, I can't do, that's how I get to do them.

**Pablo Picasso**

If you see ten troubles coming down the road, you can be sure that nine will run into the ditch before they reach you.

**Calvin Coolidge**

Positive thinking is the key to success in business, education, pro football, anything that you can mention. I go out there thinking that I'm going to complete every pass.

**Ron Jaworski**

Believe it is possible to solve your problem. Tremendous things happen to the believer. So believe the answer will come. It will.

**Norman Vincent Peale**

The impossible is often the untried.

**Jim Goodwin**

The Wright brothers flew right through the smoke screen of impossibility.

**Charles F. Kettering**

What we can or cannot do, what we consider possible or impossible, is rarely a function of our true capability. It is more likely a function of our beliefs about who we are.

**Anthony Robbins**

One must have the adventurous daring to accept oneself as a bundle of possibilities and undertake the most interesting game in the world - making the most of one's best.

**Harry Emerson Fosdick**

When a distinguished but elderly scientist states that something is possible, he is almost certainly right. When he states that something is impossible, he is very probably wrong.

**Arthur C. Clarke**

Deep within man dwell those slumbering powers; powers that would astonish him, that he never dreamed of possessing; forces that would revolutionize his life if aroused and put into action.

**Orison Swett Marsden**

I cannot discover that anyone knows enough to say definitely what is and what is not possible.

**Henry Ford**

Music expresses that which cannot be put into words and that which cannot remain silent.

**Victor Hugo**

Where words fail, music speaks.

**Hans Christian Andersen**

All the sounds of the earth are like music.

**Hans Christian Andersen**

Great music is that which penetrates the ear with facility and leaves the memory with difficulty. Magical music never leaves the memory.

**Sir Thomas Beecham**

Without music, life is a journey through a desert.

**Pat Conroy**

My father said: "You must never try to make all the money that's in a deal. Let the other fellow make some money too, because if you have a reputation for always making all the money, you won't have many deals.

**J. Paul Getty**

The most important trip you may take in life is meeting people half way.

**Henry Boyle**

Never cut what you can untie.

**Joseph Joubert**

Stand up to your obstacles and do something about them. You will find that they haven't half the strength you think they have.

**Norman Vincent Peale**

We are built to conquer environment, solve problems, achieve goals, and we find no real satisfaction or happiness in life without obstacles to conquer and goals to achieve.

**Maxwell Maltz**

As long as a man stands in his own way, everything seems to be in his way.

**Ralph Waldo Emerson**

It's the constant and determined effort that breaks down all resistance, sweeps away all obstacles.

**Claude M. Bristol**

---

You cannot escape the responsibility of tomorrow by evading it today.

**Abraham Lincoln**

Patience and perseverance have a magical effect before which difficulties disappear and obstacles vanish.

**John Quincy Adams**

Be a Columbus to whole new continents and worlds within you, opening new channels, not of trade, but of thought.

**Henry David Thoreau**

Let your hook be always cast; in the pool where you least expect it, there will be a fish.

**Ovid**

A second ago is gone, and a second from now might be. Now is all you've got. Go for it!

**Lyn St. James**

Men who are resolved to find a way for themselves will always find opportunities enough; and if they do not find them, they will make them.

**Samuel Smiles**

You are, at this moment, standing, right in the middle of your own "acres of diamonds."

**Earl Nightingale**

Not knowing when the dawn will come, I open every door.

**Emily Dickinson**

Start where you are. Distant fields always look greener, but opportunity lies right where you are. Take advantage of every opportunity of service.

**Robert Collier**

---

Nothing is more expensive than a missed opportunity.

**H. Jackson Brown Jr.**

Don't wait for extraordinary opportunities. Seize common occasions and make them great. Weak men wait for opportunities; strong men make them.

**Orison Swett Marsden**

There will always be a frontier where there is an open mind and a willing hand.

**Charles F. Kettering**

It still holds true that man is most uniquely human when he turns obstacles into opportunities.

**Eric Hoffer**

Every morning is a fresh beginning. Every day is the world made new. Today is a new day. Today is my world made new. I have lived all my life up to this moment, to come to this day. This moment - this day - is as good as any moment in all eternity. I shall make of this day - each moment of this day - a heaven on earth. This is my day of opportunity.

**Dan Custer**

The right man is the one who seizes the moment.

**Johann Wolfgang Von Goethe**

He who refuses to embrace a unique opportunity loses the prize as surely as if he had failed.

**William James**

Within our dreams and aspirations we find our opportunities.

**Sue Atchley Ebaugh**

The world is round and the place which may seem like the end may also be only the beginning.

**Ivy Baker**

Though no one can go back and make a brand new start, anyone can start from now and make a brand new ending.

**Carl Bard**

There will come a time when you believe everything is finished. That will be the beginning.

**Louis L'Amour**

People with goals succeed because they know where they are going ... It's as simple as that.

**Earl Nightingale**

The reason so many people never get anywhere in life is because when opportunity knocks, they are out in the backyard looking for four-leaf clovers.

**Walter Percy Chrysler**

You just don't luck into things as much as you'd like to think you do. You build step by step, whether it's friendships or opportunities.

**Barbara Bush**

Life has no limitations, except the ones you make.

**Les Brown**

Yesterday ended last night. Every day is a new beginning. Learn the skill of forgetting. And move on.

**Norman Vincent Peale**

Opportunities multiply as they are seized.

**Sun Tzu**

Expect nothing; be prepared for anything.

**Samurai Saying**

We will often find compensation if we think more of what life has given us and less about what life has taken away.

**William Barclay**

Small opportunities are often the beginning of great enterprises.

**Demosthenes**

Opportunity dances with those who are already on the dance floor.

**H. Jackson Brown Jr.**

People are always blaming their circumstances for what they are. I don't believe in circumstances. The people who get on in this world are the people who get up and look for the circumstances they want, and if they can't find them, make them.

**George Bernard Shaw**

# Chapter 11

There is no security on this earth, there is only opportunity.

**General Douglas MacArthur**

Opportunities are usually disguised as hard work, so most people don't recognize them.

**Ann Landers**

Luck favors the mind that is prepared.

**Louis Pasteur**

A wise man will make more opportunities than he finds.

**Francis Bacon**

Great lives are the culmination of great thoughts followed by great actions.

**Peter Sinclair**

We are new every day.

**Irene Claremont de Castillego**

Wherever there is danger, there lurks opportunity; whenever there is opportunity, there lurks danger. The two are inseparable. They go together.

**Earl Nightingale**

To see what is right and not do it, is want of courage.

**Confucius**

Courage is knowing what not to fear.

**Plato**

Men of action are favored by the Goddess of luck.

**George S. Clason**

I've decided to stick with love. Hate is too great a burden to bear.

**Martin Luther King, Jr.**

The greatest test of courage on the earth is to bear defeat without losing heart.

**R. G. Ingersoll**

Courage is what it takes to stand up and speak; courage is also what it takes to sit down and listen.

**Winston Churchill**

Thinking is easy, acting is difficult, and to put one's thoughts into action is the most difficult thing in the world.

**Goethe**

Every man has his own courage, and is betrayed because he seeks in himself the courage of other people.

**Ralph Waldo Emerson**

It is curious that physical courage should be so common in the world and moral courage so rare.

**Mark Twain**

Avoiding danger is no safer in the long run than outright exposure. Life is either a daring adventure, or nothing.

**Helen Keller**

Keep your fears to yourself, but share your courage with others.

**Robert Louis Stevenson**

Until one is committed, there is always hesitancy, the chance to draw back, always ineffectiveness. Concerning all acts of initiative (and creation), there is one element of truth, the ignorance of which kills countless ideas and splendid plans - that moment one commits oneself, then providence moves all.

**Johann von Goethe (1749-1832) German Poet and Dramatist**

Firmness founded upon principle, upon truth and right, order and law, duty and generosity, is the obstinacy of sages.

**Johann Lavater**

I have found that the greatest help in meeting any problem with decency and self-respect and whatever courage is demanded, is to know where you yourself stand. That is, to have in words what you believe and are acting from.

**William Faulkner (1897-1962) American Writer**

To think we are able is almost to be so; to determine upon attainment is frequently attainment itself; earnest resolution has often seemed to have about it almost a savor of omnipotence.

**Samuel Smiles**

To love what you do and feel that it matters -- how could anything be more fun?

**Katharine Graham (1917-2001)**

The most important thing I have learned over the years is the difference between taking one's work seriously and taking one's self seriously. The first is imperative, and the second disastrous.

**Margaret Fontey**

He who every morning plans out the transactions of the day and follows out that plan carries a thread that will guide him through the labyrinth of the most busy life.

**Victor Hugo (1802-1885) French Writer**

A professional is someone who can do his best work when he doesn't feel like it.

**Alistair Cooke (1906-) British Journalist, Television Host**

Pray for a task that will call forth your faith, your courage, your perseverance, and your spirit of sacrifice. Keep your hands and your soul clean, and the conquering spirit will flow freely.

**Thomas Dreier**

It is better to lay your life upon the altar of worthy endeavor than to luxuriate and perish as a weed.

**Albert L. Williams**

I come to the office each morning and stay for long hours doing what has to be done to the best of my ability. And when you've done the best you can you can't do any better.

**Harry S. Truman**

I'm a great believer in luck, and I find the harder I work the more I have of it.

**Thomas Jefferson (1743-1826) Third President of the United States**

Employment gives health, sobriety, and morals. Constant employment and well-paid labor produce general prosperity, content, and cheerfulness.

**Daniel Webster**

To travel hopefully is a better thing than to arrive, and the true success is to labor.

**Robert Louis Stevenson (1850-1894) Scottish Novelist**

I don't like work... but I like what is in work -- the chance to find yourself. Your own reality -- for yourself, not for others -- which no other man can ever know.

**Joseph Conrad**

No man is born into the world, whose work is not born with him. There is always work and tools to work withal, for those who will: and blessed are the horny hands of toil.

**J.R. Lowell**

Blessed is the man who has found his work; let him ask no other blessedness.

**Thomas Carlyle (1795-1881) Scottish Writer**

Determine never to be idle. No person will have occasion to complain of the want of time who never loses any. It is wonderful how much can be done if we are always doing - advising his daughter Martha, 1787.

**Thomas Jefferson (1743-1826) Third President of the United States**

Every man's work, whether it be literature or music or pictures or architecture or anything else, is always a portrait of himself.

**Samuel Butler (1835-1902) English Writer**

Enthusiasm in our daily work lightens effort and turns even labor into pleasant tasks.

**Stanley Baldwin**

A man may have as much wisdom in the possession of an affluent fortune as any beggar in the streets, or may enjoy as handsome wife or a hearty friend and still remain as wise as any sour popish recluse who buries all his social faculties and starves his belly while he well lashes his back.

**Henry Fielding (1707-1754) British Playwright and Novelist**

The art of being wise is the art of knowing what to overlook.

**William James (1842-1910) American Philosopher and Psychologist**

We must combine the toughness of the serpent with the softness of the dove, a tough mind with a tender heart.

**Martin Luther King, Jr. (1929-1968)**

Grant me the serenity to accept the things I cannot change, the courage to change the things I can and the wisdom to know the difference.

**Reinhold Niebuhr**

I shall adopt new views as fast as they shall appear to be true views.

**Abraham Lincoln (1809-1865) 16th President of the United States**

I feel sorry for the person who can't get genuinely excited about his work. Not only will he never be satisfied, but he will never achieve anything worthwhile.

**Walter Chrysler**

The key that unlocks energy is desire. It's also the key to a long and interesting life. If we expect to create any drive, any real force within ourselves, we have to get excited.

**Earl Nightingale**

Dreams get you into the future and add excitement to the present.

**Robert Conklin**

Money was never a big motivation for me, except as a way to keep score. The real excitement is playing the game.

**Donald Trump**

It is always with excitement that I wake up in the morning wondering what my intuition will toss up to me, like gifts from the sea. I work with it and rely on it. It's my partner.

**Dr. Jonas Salk**

We have forty million reasons for failure, but not a single excuse.

**Rudyard Kipling**

Nothing is impossible; there are ways that lead to everything, and if we had sufficient will we should always have sufficient means. It is often merely for an excuse that we say things are impossible.

**Francois De La Rochefoucauld**

The best job goes to the person who can get it done without passing the buck or coming back with excuses.

**Napoleon Hill**

He who excuses himself, accuses himself.

**Gabriel Meurier**

We are all manufacturers. Making good, making trouble, or making excuses.

**H. V. Adolt**

An excuse is worse than a lie, for an excuse is a lie, guarded.

**Alexander Pope**

Bad excuses are worse than none.

**Thomas Fuller**

He that is good for making excuses is seldom good for anything else.

**Benjamin Franklin**

By asking for the impossible we obtain the best possible.

**Giovanni Niccolini**

Don't believe in miracles - depend on them.

**Laurence J. Peter**

We usually get what we anticipate.

**Claude M. Bristol**

Few enterprises of great labor or hazard would be undertaken if we had not the power of magnifying the advantages we expect from them.

**Samuel Johnson**

Live your beliefs and you can turn the world around.

**Henry David Thoreau**

What we see depends mainly on what we look for.

**John Lubbock**

High expectations are the key to everything.

**Sam Walton**

Look and you will find it. What is unsought will go undetected.

**Sophocles**

Man often becomes what he believes himself to be. If I keep on saying to myself that I cannot do a certain thing, it is possible that I may end by really becoming incapable of doing it. On the contrary, if I have the belief that I can do it, I shall surely acquire the capacity to do it even if I may not have it at the beginning.

**Mahatma Gandhi**

You will never be happier than you expect. To change your happiness, change your expectation.

**Bette Davis**

Expect your every need to be met. Expect the answer to every problem, expect abundance on every level.

**Eileen Caddy**

A people that values its privileges above its principles soon loses both.

**Dwight D. Eisenhower**

A better world shall emerge based on faith and understanding.

**Douglass MacArthur**

The truth of the matter is that you always know the right thing to do. The hard part is doing it.

**Norman Schwarzkopf**

Neither a wise nor a brave man lies down on the tracks of history to wait for the train of the future to run over him.

**Dwight D. Eisenhower**

We need to learn to set our course by the stars, not by the lights of every passing ship.

**Omar Nelson Bradley**

If a man does his best, what else is there?

**General George S. Patton**

Only our individual faith in freedom can keep us free.

**Dwight D. Eisenhower**

Some people wanted champagne and caviar when they should have had beer and hot dogs.

**Dwight D. Eisenhower**

My responsibility, our responsibility as lucky Americans, is to try to give back to this country as much as it has given us, as we continue our American journey together.

**Colin Powell**

When placed in command -- take charge.

**Norman Schwarzkopf**

I have nothing to offer but blood, toil, tears, and sweat.

**Winston Churchill**

We succeed only as we identify in life, or in war, or in anything else, a single overriding objective, and make all other considerations bend to that one objective.

**Dwight D. Eisenhower**

Lead me, follow me, or get out of my way.

**George Patton**

There is no security on this earth, there is only opportunity.

**Douglas McArthur**

Leadership is the art of getting someone else to do something you want done because he wants to do it.

**Dwight Eisenhower**

Live for something rather than die for nothing.

**George Patton**

Leadership is a potent combination of strategy and character. But if you must be without one, be without the strategy.

**Norman Schwarzkopf**

When you are in any contest you should work as if there were - to the very last minute - a chance to lost it.

**Dwight D. Eisenhower**

Every gun that is made, every warship launched, every rocket fired signifies, in the final sense, a theft from those who hunger and are not fed, those who are cold and not clothed.

**Dwight D. Eisenhower**

The best morale exists when you never hear the word mentioned. When you hear it it's usually lousy.

**Dwight D. Eisenhower**

---

If everybody is thinking alike, then somebody isn't thinking.

**George S. Patton**

There is a time to take counsel of your fears, and there is a time to never listen to any fear.

**George S. Patton**

I think we consider too much the good luck of the early bird and not enough the bad luck of the early worm.

**Theodore Roosevelt**

Character is like a tree and a reputation like a shadow. The shadow is what we think of it; the tree is the real thing.

**Abraham Lincoln**

Opportunity is missed by most people because it is dressed in overalls and looks like work.

**Thomas Edison**

The only man who make no mistakes is the man who never does anything.

**Theodore Roosevelt**

I do not know beneath what sky nor on what seas shall be thy fate; I only know it shall be high, I only know it shall be great.

**Richard Hovey**

There is no chance, no destiny, no fate, that can hinder or control the firm resolve of a determined soul.

**Ella Wheeler Wilcox**

Men are not prisoners of fate, but only prisoners of their own minds.

**Franklin D. Roosevelt**

Man's character is his fate.

**Heraclitus**

There is but one philosophy and its name is fortitude! To bear is to conquer our fate.

**Edward G. Bulwer-Lytton**

Most people have no idea of the giant capacity we can immediately command when we focus all of our resources on mastering a single area of our lives.

**Anthony Robbins**

The immature mind hops from one thing to another; the mature mind seeks to follow through.

**Harry A. Overstreet**

Every man's life lies within the present; for the past is spent and done with, and the future is uncertain.

**Marcus Aurelius**

Only when your consciousness is totally focused on the moment you are in can you receive whatever gift, lesson, or delight that moment has to offer.

**Barbara De Angelis**

Often he who does too much does too little.

**Italian Proverb**

If you focus on results, you will never change. If you focus on change, you will get results.

**Jack Dixon**

Concentration is the secret of strengths in politics, in war, in trade, in short in all management of human affairs.

**Ralph Waldo Emerson**

The indispensable first step to getting the things you want out of life is this: decide what you want.

**Ben Stein**

The truly important things in life -- love, beauty, and one's own uniqueness -- are constantly being overlooked.

**Pablo Casals**

You can't pick cherries with your back to the tree.

**John Pierpont (J.P.) Morgan**

Concentrate all your thoughts upon the work at hand. The sun's rays do not burn until brought to a focus.

**Alexander Graham Bell**

The main thing is keeping the main thing the main thing.

**German Proverb**

I never see what has been done; I only see what remains to be done.

**Marie Curie**

It's the constant and determined effort that breaks down resistance, sweeps away all obstacles.

**Claude M. Bristol**

A man of sense is never discouraged by difficulties; he redoubles his industry and his diligence, he perseveres and infallibly prevails at last.

**Lord Chesterfield**

I just try to be the best I can be and hope that is the best ever.

**Tiger Woods**

Don't let the mistakes and disappointments of the past control and direct your future.

**Zig Ziglar**

To get what you want. STOP doing what isn't working.

**Dennis Weaver**

I want to put a ding in the universe.

**Steve Jobs**

You can't depend on your judgment when your imagination is out of focus.

**Mark Twain**

Nothing interferes with my concentration. You could put an orgy in my office and I wouldn't look up. Well, maybe once.

**Isaac Asimov**

Paying attention to simple little things that most men neglect makes a few men rich.

**Henry Ford**

Beware lest you lose the substance by grasping at the shadow.

**Aesop**

Look and you will find it - what is unsought will go undetected.

**Sophocles**

Focus on where you want to go, not on what you fear.

**Anthony Robbins**

Do the hard jobs first. The easy jobs will take care of themselves.

**Dale Carnegie**

Success is simple. Do what's right, the right way, at the right time.

**Arnold Glascow**

Don't aim for success if you want it; just do what you love and believe in, and it will come naturally.

**David Frost**

It's simply a matter of doing what you do best and not worrying about what the other fellow is going to do.

**John Adams**

Some people think they are concentrating when they're merely worrying.

**Bobby Jones**

Only that day dawns to which we are awake.

**Henry David Thoreau**

Correct one fault at a time. Concentrate on the one fault you want to overcome.

**Sam Snead**

All that we are is the result of what we have thought.

**Buddha**

What we see depends mainly on what we look for.

**Sir John Lubbock**

I just try to concentrate on concentrating.

**Martina Navratilova**

Act the part and you will become the part.

**William James**

Confidence is a lot of this game or any game. If you don't think you can, you won't.

**Jerry West**

I have simply tried to do what seemed best each day, as each day came.
**Abraham Lincoln**

Common sense is the knack of seeing things as they are, and doing things as they ought to be done.
**Harriet Beecher Stowe (1811-1896) American Novelist**

A man should never be ashamed to own that he has been in the wrong, which is but saying that he is wiser today than he was yesterday.
**Alexander Pope (1688-1744) English Poet**

Describing the trance into which the average American had fallen by the summer of 1929: He visioned an America set free from poverty and toil. He saw a magical order built on the new science and the new prosperity: roads swarming with millions upon millions of automobiles, airplanes darkening the skies, lines of high-tension wire carrying from hilltop to hilltop the power to give life to a thousand labor saving machines, skyscrapers thrusting above one-time villages, vast cities rising in great geometrical masses of stone and concrete and roaring with perfectly mechanized traffic - and smartly dressed men and women spending, spending the money they had won by being far-sighted enough to forsee, way back in 1929, what was going to happen.
**Frederick Lewis Allen**

The potential of the average person is like a huge ocean unsailed, a new continent unexplored, a world of possibilities waiting to be released and channeled toward some great good.

**Brian Tracy**

I was told over and over again that I would never be successful, that I was not going to be competitive and the technique was simply not going to work. All I could do was shrug and say "We'll just have to see."
**Dick Fosbury, who won an Olympic gold medal at the 1968 Mexico games after he invented a revolutionary high-jump technique.**

---

Life is no brief candle to me. It is sort of a splendid torch which I have got hold of for a moment, and I want to make it burn as brightly as possible before handing it on to future generations.

**George Bernard Shaw (1856-1950) Irish Playwright**

People with goals succeed because they know where they are going ... it's as simple as that.

**Earl Nightingale**

Blessed is he who carries within himself a God, an ideal, and obeys it.

**Louis Pasteur (1822-1895) French Scientist**

You see things; and you say, "Why?" But I dream things that never were; and I say "Why not?"

**George Bernard Shaw (1856-1950) Irish Playwright**

Tears are often the telescope by which men see far into heaven.

**Henry Ward Beecher (1813-1887) American Presbyterian Minister**

Beauty in things exists in the mind which contemplates them.

**David Hume (1711-1776) Scottish Philosopher and Historian**

When a distinguished but elderly scientist states that something is possible, he is almost certainly right. When he states that something is impossible, he is very probably wrong.

**Arthur C. Clarke (1917-) British Science Fiction Writer**

They are ill discoverers that think there is no land, when they can see nothing but sea.

**Francis Bacon (1561-1626) English Philosopher,**
**Lawyer and Politician**

God could not be everywhere, so he created mothers.

**Jewish proverb**

# Chapter 12

You cannot do a kindness too soon, for you never know how soon it will be too late.

**Ralph Waldo Emerson (1803-1882) American Poet and Essayist**

The ideas that have lighted my way have been kindness, beauty and truth.

**Albert Einstein (1879-1955) German-American Physicist**

The man who succeeds above his fellows is the one who early in life clearly discerns his object, and towards that object habitually directs his powers.

**Earl Nightingale**

There is overwhelming evidence that the higher the level of self-esteem, the more likely one will be to treat others with respect, kindness, and generosity.

**Nathaniel Branden (1930-) American Author and Psychologist**

Knowing sorrow well, I learn to succor the distressed.

**Virgil (Publius Vergilius Maro) (70-19BC) Latin Poet**

Wise sayings often fall on barren ground, but a kind word is never thrown away.

**Arthur Helps (1813-1875) English Historian and Novelist**

Be kind, for everyone you meet is fighting a battle.

**John Watson (1867-1941) Australian Prime Minister**

You have it easily in your power to increase the sum total of this world's happiness now. How? By giving a few words of sincere appreciation to someone who is lonely or discouraged.

**Dale Carnegie (1888-1955) American Author and Speaker**

If you have not often felt the joy of doing a kind act, you have neglected much, and most of all yourself.

**A. Neilen**

Kindness is the language which the deaf can hear and the blind can see.
**Mark Twain (b: Samuel Langhorne Clemens) (1835-1910)**
**American Author and Humorist**

The best portion of a good man's life is the little, nameless, unremembered acts of kindness and love.
**William Wordsworth (1770-1850) English poet**

So great has been the endurance, so incredible the achievement, that, as long as the sun keeps a set course in heaven, it would be foolish to despair of the human race.

**Ernest L. Woodward**

Dum spiro spero. (While I breathe I hope.)
**Lindsay clan Family motto (Scotland)**

He who has health has hope; and he who has hope, has everything.
**Arabian Proverb**

If I were to wish for anything, I should not wish for wealth and power, but for the passionate sense of the potential, for the eye which, ever young and ardent, sees the possible...what wine is so sparkling, so fragrant, so intoxicating, as possibility!
**Soren Aabye Kierkagaard (1813-1855) Danish Philosopher**

Hope is a feeling that life and work have meaning. You either have it or you don't, regardless of the state of the world which surrounds you.... I can't imagine that I could strive for something if I did not carry hope in me. The gift of hope is as big a gift as life itself.

**Vaclav Havel (1936-) Czech President**

Hope sees the invisible, feels the intangible, and achieves the impossible.

**Charles Caleb Colton (1780-1832) English Author and Clergyman**

In the lexicon of youth, which fate reserves for a bright manhood, there is no such word as Fail.

**Owen Meredith**

I don't fear failure. I only fear the slowing up of the engine inside of me which is saying, "Keep going, someone must be on top, why not you?"

**George S. Patton**

If I have ever made any valuable discoveries, it has been owing more to patient attention than to any other talent.

**Isaac Newton (1642-1727) English Scientist**

Genius is eternal patience.

**Michelangelo Di Lodovico Buonarroti Simoni (1475-1564) Italian Sculptor and Painter**

Patience is passion tamed.

**Lyman Abbott**

I'm not happy, I'm cheerful. There's a difference. A happy woman has no cares at all. A cheerful woman has cares but has learned how to deal with them.

**Beverly Sills (1929-) American Opera Singer**

Happiness is essentially a state of going somewhere, wholeheartedly, one-directionally, without regret or reservation.

**William H. Sheldon**

He felt that he could forgive anything to anyone, because happiness was the greatest agent of purification.

**Ayn Rand (1905-1982) Russian-American Writer and Philosopher**

What a man is contributes much more to his happiness than what he has, or how he is regarded by others.

**Arthur Schopenhauer**

One's true happiness depends more upon one's own judgment of one's self, on a consciousness of rectitude in action and intention, and in the approbation of those few who judge impartially, than upon the applause of the unthinking undiscerning multitude, who are apt to cry Hosanna today, and tomorrow, Crucify him.

**Benjamin Franklin**

True happiness is not attained through self-gratification, but through fidelity to a worthy purpose.

**Helen Keller (1880-1968) American Writer**

To make a man happy, fill his hands with work, his heart with affection, his mind with purpose, his memory with useful knowledge, his future with hope, and his stomach with food.

**Frederick E. Crane**

The world is good-natured to people who are good natured.

**William Makepeace Thackeray**

What's really important in life? Sitting on a beach? Looking at television eight hours a day? I think we have to appreciate that we're alive for only a limited period of time, and we'll spend most of our lives working. That being the case, I believe one of the most important priorities is to do whatever we do as well as we can. We should take pride in that.

**Victor Kiam**

What can be added to the happiness of a man who is in health, out of debt, and has a clear conscience?

**Adam Smith (1723-1790)**

Happiness is like a cat. If you try to coax it or call it, it will avoid you. It will never come. But if you pay no attention to it and go about your business, you'll find it rubbing up against your legs and jumping into your lap.

**(Dr.) William (J.) Bennett (1943- )**
**American Author and Educator**

Effort only fully releases its reward after a person refuses to quit.

**Napoleon Hill**

Who is the happiest of men? He who values the merits of others, and in their pleasure takes joy, even as though t'were his own.

**Johann von Goethe (1749-1832) German Poet and Dramatist**

The grand essentials to happiness in this life are something to do, something to love and something to hope for.

**Joseph Addison (1672–1719) English Writer and Statesman**

No pleasure philosophy, no sensuality, no place nor power, no material success can for a moment give such inner satisfaction as the sense of living for good purposes, for maintenance of integrity, for the preservation of self-approval.

**Minot Simons**

Look to your health; and if you have it, praise God and value it next to conscience; for health is the second blessing that we mortals are capable of, a blessing money can't buy.

**Izaak Walton**

Most people never run far enough on their first wind to find out they've got a second. Give your dreams all you've got and you'll be amazed at the energy that comes out of you.

**William James**

A good beginning makes a good end.

**English Proverb**

No matter what business you're in, you can't run in place or someone will pass you by. It doesn't matter how many games you've won.

**Jim Valvano**

Little by little does the trick.

**Aesop**

Do every act of your life as if it were your last.

**Marcus Aurelius**

Folks who never do any more than they get paid for, never get paid for any more than they do.

**Elbert Hubbard**

The one thing that matters is the effort.

**Antoine De Saint-Exupery**

Every day do something that will inch you closer to a better tomorrow.

**Doug Firebaugh**

Where you start is not as important as where you finish.

**Zig Ziglar**

Do a little more each day than you think you can.

**Lowell Thomas**

Satisfaction lies in the effort, not in the attainment. Full effort is full victory.

**Mohandas Gandhi**

One must learn by doing the thing, for though you think you know it, you have no certainty until you try.

**Aristotle**

Apply yourself. Get all the education you can, but then, by God, do something. Don't just stand there, make it happen.

**Lee Iacocca**

So many fail because they don't get started - they don't go. They don't overcome inertia. They don't begin.

**W. Clement Stone**

I have been impressed with the urgency of doing. Knowing is not enough; we must apply. Being willing is not enough; we must do.

**Russell C. Taylor**

If you shoot for the stars and hit the moon, it's OK. But you've got to shoot for something. A lot of people don't even shoot.

**Robert Townsend**

One may walk over the highest mountain one step at a time.

**John Wanamaker**

I've got all the money I'll ever need, if I die by four o'clock.

**Henny Youngman**

You don't have to be great to start, but you have to start to be great.

**Zig Ziglar**

You must not only aim right, but draw the bow with all your might.

**Henry David Thoreau**

Do not wait; the time will never be 'just right'. Start where you stand, and work with whatever tools you may have at your command, and better tools will be found as you go along.

**Napoleon Hill**

Life is like riding a bike. It is impossible to maintain your balance while standing still.

**Linda Brakeall**

Motivation is what gets you started. Habit is what keeps you going.

**Jim Ryan**

One that would have the fruit must climb the tree.

**Thomas Fuller**

We are what we repeatedly do. Excellence, then, is not an act, but a habit.

**Aristotle**

It doesn't take talent to hustle.

**H. Jackson Brown**

It's blood, sweat, sometimes tears.

**Bob Hayes**

Everything in space obeys the laws of physics. If you know these laws and obey them, space will treat you kindly. And don't tell me that man doesn't belong out there. Man belongs wherever he wants to go; and he'll do plenty well when he gets there.

**Vernher von Braun, German rocket engineer who came to the U.S. to work on the space program. Quoted in Time Magazine, February, 1958.**

The happiness of your life depends on the quality of your thoughts: therefore, guard accordingly, and take care that you entertain no notions unsuitable to virtue and reasonable nature.

**Theodore Roosevelt (1858-1919) 26th President of the United States**

We are fallible. We certainly haven't attained perfection. But we can strive for it, and the virtue is in the striving.

**Carlos P. Romulo (1899-1985) Phillipine Diplomat, Aide-de-camp to Gen. Douglas MacArthur**

The important thing is this: to be able at any moment to sacrifice what we are for what we could become.

**Charles Du Bos**

The true men of action in our time, those who transform the world, are not the politicians and statesmen, but the scientists.

**W. H. Auden (1907-1973) British Poet**

Man is still responsible... His success lies not with the stars but with himself. He must carry on the fight of self-correction and discipline. He must fight mediocrity as sin and live against the imperative of life's highest ideal.

**Frank Curtis Williams**

On the whole, despite pollution, resource recklessness and waste, I'm glad of the boom. I'm glad that people I know can move out of two-roomed damp gardenless slums into three-bed roomed council houses with bathrooms and lawns.... I'm glad that the sons are six inches taller than the fathers and that their sons show signs even of overtopping them.

**Melvyn Bragg (1939-) British Writer and Broadcaster**

The tough-minded... respect difference. Their goal is a world made safe for differences, where the United States may be American to the hilt without threatening the peace of the world, and France may be France, and Japan may be Japan on the same conditions.

**Pearl S. Buck (1892-1963) American Writer**

People call me an optimist, but I'm really an appreciator....When I was six years old and had scarlet fever, the first of the miracle drugs, sulfanilamide, saved my life. I'm grateful for computers and photocopiers...I appreciate where we've come from.

**Julian Simon (1933-1998) American Academic**

You are today where your thoughts have brought you, you will be tomorrow where your thoughts take you.

**James Allen**

The great German poet, Goethe, who also lived through a crisis of freedom, said to his generation: "What you have inherited from your fathers, earn over again for yourselves or it will not be yours." We inherited freedom. We seem unaware that freedom has to be remade and re-earned in each generation of man.

**Adlai Stevenson**

The wonder is, not that the field of stars is so vast, but that man has measured it.

**Anatole France (1844-1924) French Poet, Novelist and Critic**

Every heart that has beat strongly and cheerfully has left a hopeful impulse behind it in the world, and bettered the tradition of mankind.

**Robert Louis Stevenson (1850-1894) Scottish Novelist**

Progress in every age results only from the fact that there are some men and women who refuse to believe that what they know to be right cannot be done.

**Russell W. Davenport - American Editor, Fortune Magazine**

It is more important to know where you are going than to get there quickly.

**Mabel Newcomber**

Despite some of the horrors and barbarisms of modern life which appall and grieve us, life has - or has the potential of - such richness, joy and adventure as were unknown to our ancestors except in their dreams.

**Arthur Holly Compton (1892-1962) American Physicist**

Little progress can be made by merely attempting to repress what is evil; our great hope lies in developing what is good.

**Calvin Coolidge**

Few will have the greatness to bend history itself, but each one of us can work to change a small portion of events, and in the total of all those acts will be written the history of this generation.

**Robert F. Kennedy (1925-1968)**
**American Attorney General, Senator**

You can't climb up to the second floor without a ladder. When you set your aim too high and don't fulfill it, then your enthusiasm turns to bitterness. Try for a goal that's reasonable, and then gradually raise it. That's the only way to get to the top.

**Emil Zatopek (1922-) Czech Middle Distance Runner**

I have resolved from this day on, I will do all the business I can honestly, have all the fun I can reasonably, do all the good I can willingly, and save my digestion by thinking pleasantly.

**Robert Louis Stevenson (1850-1894) Scottish Novelist**

Have the courage and the wisdom and the vision to raise a definite standard that will appeal to the best that is in man, and then strive mightily toward that goal.

**Harold E. Stassen**

---

Despite the success cult, men are most deeply moved not by the reaching of the goal, but by the grandness of the effort involved in getting there.
**Max Lerner (1902-1992) American Educator, Columnist**

Let no man turn aside, ever so slightly, from the broad path of honor, on the plausible pretence that he is justified by the goodness of his end. All good ends can be worked out by good means.
**Charles Dickens (1812-1870) English Novelist**

A goal is a dream that has an ending.
**Duke (Edward Kennedy) Ellington (1899-1974)**
**American Composer Bandleader and Pianist**

Do not dare to live without some clear intention toward which your living shall be bent. Mean to be something with all your might.
**Phillips Brooks (1835-1893) American Bishop**

Slight not what is near though aiming at what is far.
**Euripides (480-406 BC) Greek Playwright**

I don't think anything is unrealistic if you believe you can do it. I think if you are determined enough and willing to pay the price, you can get it done.
**Mike Ditka (1939-) American, Football Coach, Chicago Bears**

Aspire, break bounds. Endeavor to be good, and better still, best.
**Robert Browning**

The force is within you. Force yourself.
**Harrison Ford (1942-) American Actor**

Everyone who has ever taken a shower has had an idea. It's the person who gets out of the shower, dries off, and does something about it that makes a difference.

**Nolan Bushnell**

Diligence is the mother of good luck.

**Benjamin Franklin**

The expectations of life depend upon diligence; the mechanic that would perfect his work must first sharpen his tools.

**Confucius**

Few things are impossible to diligence and skill. Great works are performed not by strength, but perseverance.

**Samuel Johnson**

Diligence is the mother of good fortune, and idleness, its opposite, never brought a man to the goal of any of his best wishes.

**Miguel De Cervantes**

I have had dreams, and I have had nightmares. I overcame the nightmares because of my dreams.

**Dr. Jonas Salk**

You have all the reason in the world to achieve your grandest dreams. Imagination plus innovation equals realization.

**Denis Waitley**

Man, alone, has the power to transform his thoughts into physical reality; man, alone, can dream and make his dreams come true.

**Napolean Hill**

Dream big and dare to fail.

**Norman D. Vaughan**

Build a dream and the dream will build you.

**Robert H. Schuller**

It may be those who do most, dream most.

**Stephen B. Leacock**

I will! I am! I can! I will actualize my dream. I will press ahead. I will settle down and see it through. I will solve the problems. I will pay the price. I will never walk away from my dream until I see my dream walk away: Alert! Alive! Achieved!

**Robert Schuller**

If you have built castles in the air, your work need not be lost; that is where they should be. Now put the foundations under them.

**Henry David Thoreau**

When you cease to dream you cease to live.

**Malcolm S. Forbes**

A dream is your creative vision for your life in the future. You must break out of your current comfort zone and become comfortable with the unfamiliar and the unknown.

**Denis Waitley**

Those who dream by day are cognizant of many things which escape those who dream only by night.

**Alexander Pope**

As soon as you start to pursue a dream, your life wakes up and everything has meaning.

**Barbara Sher**

Nothing happens unless first a dream.

**Carl Sandburg**

A man is not old until regrets take the place of dreams.

**John Barrymore**

You are never given a dream without also being given the power to make it true. You may have to work for it, however.

**Richard Bach**

If you don't have a dream, how are you going to make a dream come true?

**Oscar Hammerstein**

We grow great by dreams. All big men are dreamers.

**Woodrow T. Wilson**

The problems of this world cannot possibly be solved by skeptics or cynics whose horizons are limited by the obvious realities. We need men who can dream of things that never were.

**John F. Kennedy**

# *Chapter 13*

Use what talents you possess; The woods would be very silent if no birds sang there except those that sang best.

**Henry Van Dyke**

I could never convince the financiers that Disneyland was feasible because dreams offer too little collateral.

**Walt Disney**

Dreams do come true, if we only wish hard enough, you can have anything in life if you will sacrifice everything else for it.

**Sir James M. Barrie**

Keep your dreams alive. Understand to achieve anything requires faith and belief in yourself, vision, hard work, determination, and dedication. Remember all things are possible for those who believe.

**Gail Devers**

To accomplish great things, we must not only act, but also dream; not only plan, but also believe.

**Anatole France**

There are some people who live in a dream world, and there are some who face reality; and then there are those who turn one into the other.

**Douglas Everett**

A bird doesn't sing because it has an answer, it sings because it has a song.

**Maya Angelou**

Every great and commanding movement in the annals of the world is the triumph of enthusiasm.

**Ralph Waldo Emerson**

"HAPPINESS"

One way to become enthusiastic is to look for the plus sign. To make progress in any difficult situation, you have to start with what's right about it and build on that.

**Norman Vincent Peale**

Enthusiasm is the yeast that raises the dough.

**Paul J. Meyer**

Years wrinkle the skin, but to give up enthusiasm wrinkles the soul.

**Douglas MacArthur**

Excellence is the gradual result of always striving to do better.

**Pat Riley**

People think that at the top there isn't much room. They tend to think of it as an Everest. My message is that there is tons of room at the top.

**Margaret Thatcher**

Any thought that is passed on to the subconscious often enough and convincingly enough is finally accepted.

**Robert Collier**

Every great man is unique.

**Ralph Waldo Emerson**

The noblest search is the search for excellence.

**Lyndon B. Johnson**

To aim at excellence, our reputation, and friends, and all must be ventured; to aim at the average we run no risk and provide little service.

**Oliver Goldsmith**

Those who attain to any excellence commonly spend life in some single pursuit, for excellence is not often gained upon easier terms.

**Samuel Johnson**

I do the very best I know how - the very best I can; and I mean to keep on doing so until the end.

**Abraham Lincoln**

Whatever you do, don't do it halfway.

**Bob Beamon**

There is no victory at bargain basement prices.

**Dwight D. Eisenhower**

People forget how fast you did a job, but they remember how well you did it.

**Howard W. Newton**

Hold yourself responsible for a higher standard than anybody expects of you. Never excuse yourself.

**Henry Ward Beecher**

It's unfulfilled dreams that keep you alive.

**Robert Schuller**

Discipline is the soul of an army. It makes small numbers formidable; procures success to the weak, and esteem to all.

**George Washington**

You say I started out with practically nothing, but that isn't correct. We all start with all there is. It's how we use it that makes things possible.

**Henry Ford**

Everyone is trying to accomplish something big, not realizing that life is made up of little things.

**Frank A. Clark**

Some of us let our dreams die, but others nourish and protect them, nurse them through bad days 'till they bring them to sunshine and light.

**Woodrow Wilson**

Ordinary riches can be stolen: real riches cannot. In your soul are infinitely precious things that cannot be taken from you.

**Oscar Wilde**

Initiative is to success what a lighted match is to a candle.

**Orlando A. Battista**

The fact is, that to do anything in the world worth doing, we must not stand back shivering and thinking of the cold and danger, but jump in and scramble through as well as we can.

**Robert Cushing (Robert Cushing Dennison) (1921-1998)**
**American Colonel**

The person who removes a mountain begins by carrying away small stones.

**Chinese proverb**

Obstacles cannot crush me. Every obstacle yields to stern resolve. He who is fixed to a star does not change his mind.

**Leonardo da Vinci**

Nothing in the world can take the place of persistence. Talent will not; nothing is more common than unsuccessful men with talent. Genius will not; unrewarded genius is almost a proverb. Education will not; the world is full of educated derelicts. Persistence and determination alone are omnipotent.

**Calvin Coolidge**

---

Never give in! Never give in! Never, never, never, never - in nothing great or small, large or petty. Never give in except to convictions of honor and good sense.

**Winston Churchill**

Most of the important things in the world have been accomplished by people who have kept on trying when there seemed to be no help at all.

**Dale Carnegie**

To him who is determined it remains only to act.

**Italian Proverb**

The best way out is always through.

**Robert Frost**

People are always blaming their circumstances for what they are. I don't believe in circumstances. The people who get on in the world are the people who get up and look for the circumstances they want, and if they can't find them, make them.

**George Bernard Shaw**

Every person who wins in any undertaking must be willing to cut all sources of retreat. Only by doing so can one be sure of maintaining that state of mind known as a burning desire to win - essential to success.

**Napoleon Hill**

Tough times never last, but tough people do.

**Dr. Robert Schuller**

The miracle, or the power, that elevates the few is to be found in their perseverance under the promptings of a brave, determined spirit.

**Mark Twain**

I count him braver who overcomes his desires than him who conquers his enemies; for the hardest victory is the victory over self.

**Aristotle**

Begin with the end in mind.

**Stephen Covey**

It's easier to go down a hill than up it but the view is much better at the top.

**Henry Ward Beecher**

Ambition is the germ from which all growth of nobleness proceeds.

**Thomas Dunn English**

Most of our obstacles would melt away if, instead of cowering before them, we should make up our minds to walk boldly through them.

**Orison Swett Marden**

It is common sense to take a method and try it. If it fails, admit it frankly and try another. But above all, try something.

**Franklin D Roosevelt**

Whatever you can do, or dream you can, begin it. Boldness has genius, power and magic in it.

**Johann Wolfgang Von Goethe**

Will you look back on life and say, 'I wish I had,' or 'I'm glad I did'?

**Zig Ziglar**

Never mind what others do; do better than yourself, beat your own record from day to day, and you are a success.

**William J.H. Boetcker**

Leaders aren't born, they are made. And they are made just like anything else, through hard work. And that's the price we'll have to pay to achieve that goal, or any goal.

**Vincent Lombardi**

We will either find a way, or make one.

**Hannibal**

Mind is all that counts. You can be whatever you make up your mind to be.

**Robert Collier**

Determination and perseverance move the world; thinking that others will do it for you is a sure way to fail.

**Marva Collins**

The good Lord gave you a body that can stand most anything. It's your mind you have to convince.

**Vincent Lombardi**

In nature there are neither rewards nor punishments - there are consequences.

**Robert G Ingersoll**

The future is something which everyone reaches at the rate of sixty minutes and hour, whatever he does, whoever he is.

**C.S. Lewis**

A man may fulfill the object of his existence by asking a question he cannot answer and attempting a task he cannot achieve.

**Oliver Wendall Holmes**

I was the kind nobody thought could make it. I had a funny Boston accent. I couldn't pronounce my R's. I wasn't a beauty.

**Barbara Walters**

On the mountains of truth you can never climb in vain: either you will reach a point higher up today, or you will be training your powers so that you will be able to climb higher tomorrow.

**Frederick Nietzsche**

In three words I can sum up everything I've learned about life. It goes on.

**Robert Frost**

Winning is not everything, but the effort to win is.

**Zig Ziglar**

Good work habits help develop an internal toughness and self-confident attitude that will sustain you through every adversity and temporary discouragement.

**Paul Fleyer**

Once a man has made a commitment to a way of life, he puts the greatest strength in the world behind him. It's something we call heart power. Once a man has made this commitment, nothing will stop him short of success.

**Vincent Lombardi**

Vitality shows not only in the ability to persist, but in the ability to start over.

**F. Scott Fitzgerald**

Don't give up at half time. Concentrate on winning the second half.

**Paul "Bear" Bryant**

Success is a ladder you cannot climb with your hands in our pockets.

**American Proverb**

Nobody ever drowned in his own sweat.

**Ann Landers**

---

Hard work spotlights the character of people: some turn up their sleeves, some turn up their noses, and some don't turn up at all.

**Sam Ewing**

Thinking is the hardest work there is, which is the probable reason so few engage in it.

**Henry Ford**

The more you venture to live greatly, the more you will find within you what it takes to get on top of the things and stay there.

**Norman Vincent Peale**

Do whatever it takes, whenever it needs to be done, regardless of whether you feel like doing it or not.

**Greg Hickman**

I find the great thing in this world is not so much where we stand, as in what direction we are moving: To reach the port of heaven, we must sail sometimes with the wind and sometimes against it, -- but we must sail, and not drift, nor lie at anchor.

**Oliver Wendell Holmes (1809-1894) American Writer**

The way to learn to do things is to do things. The way to learn a trade is to work at it. Success teaches how to succeed. Begin with the determination to succeed, and the work is half done already.

**J.N. Fadenburg**

The secret of getting ahead is getting started. The secret of getting started is breaking your complex overwhelming tasks into small manageable tasks, and then starting on the first one.

**Mark Twain**

The spirited horse, which will try to win the race of its own accord, will run even faster if encouraged.

**Ovid**

The vision must be followed by the venture. It is not enough to stare up the steps - We must step up the stairs.

**Vance Havner (1901-1986) American Baptist Preacher**

I am only one; but still I am one. I cannot do everything, but still I can do something; I will not refuse to do the something I can do.

**Helen Keller**

You only lose energy when life becomes dull in your mind. Your mind gets bored and therefore tired of doing nothing. Get interested in something! Get absolutely enthralled in something! Get out of yourself! Be somebody! Do something. The more you lose yourself in something bigger than yourself, the more energy you will have.

**Norman Vincent Peale**

Don't wait for your "ship to come in" and feel angry and cheated when it doesn't. Get going with something small.

**Irene Kassorla**

Nothing will ever be attempted, if all possible objections must first be overcome.

**Samuel Johnson (1709-1784) English Author**

To be able to practice five things everywhere under heaven constitutes perfect virtue... gravity, generosity of soul, sincerity, earnestness, and kindness. Confucius (551-479 BC)

**Chinese Philosopher**

Rely on the ordinary virtues that intelligent, balanced human beings have relied on for centuries: common sense, thrift, realistic expectations, patience, and perseverance.

**John C. Bogle (1929-) American Investor**

Appreciation can make a day - even change a life, Your willingness to put it into words is all that is necessary.

**Margaret Cousins**

Correction does much, but encouragement does more. Encouragement after censure is as the sun after a shower.

**Johann Wolfgang von Goethe**

Those who are lifting the world upward and onward are those who encourage more than criticize.

**Elizabeth Harrison**

Any man's life will be filled with constant and unexpected encouragement if he makes up his mind to do his level best each day.

**Booker T. Washington**

You need to be aware of what others are doing, applaud their efforts, acknowledge their successes, and encourage them in their pursuits. When we all help one another, everybody wins.

**Jim Stovall**

Note how good you feel after you have encouraged someone else. No other argument is necessary to suggest that never miss the opportunity to give encouragement.

**George Adams**

Treat people as if they were what they ought to be and you help them to become what they are capable of being.

**Johann Wolfgang von Goethe**

All the breaks you need in life wait within your imagination. Imagination is the workshop of your mind, capable of turning mind energy into accomplishment and wealth.

**Napoleon Hill**

Failure is more frequently from want of energy than want of capital.

**Daniel Webster**

Genius is that energy which collects, combines, amplifies, and animates.

**Samuel Johnson**

It is essential to our well-being, and to our lives, that we play and enjoy life. Every single day do something that makes your heart sing.

**Marcia Wieder**

Every minute should be enjoyed and savored.

**Earl Nightingale**

Be absolutely determined to enjoy what you do.

**Gerry Sikorski**

The first half of life consists of the capacity to enjoy without the chance; the last half consists of the chance without the capacity.

**Mark Twain**

As you walk down the fairway of life you must smell the roses, for you only get to play one round.

**Ben Hogan**

Enjoy the journey, enjoy ever moment, and quit worrying about winning and losing.

**Matt Biondi**

If your capacity to acquire has outstripped your capacity to enjoy, you are on the way to the scrap-heap.

**Glen Buck**

People who enjoy what they are doing invariably do it well.

**Joe Gibbs**

---

Celebrate what you want to see more of.

Thomas J. Peters

Every great and commanding movement in the annals of the world is the triumph of enthusiasm.

Ralph Waldo Emerson

To waken interest and kindle enthusiasm is the sure way to teach easily and successfully.

Tryon Edwards

A man can succeed at almost anything for which he has unlimited enthusiasm.

Charles Schwab

I found that the men and women who got to the top were those who did the jobs they had in hand, with everything they had of energy and enthusiasm and hard work.

Harry S. Truman

Enthusiasm releases the drive to carry you over obstacles and adds significance to all you do.

Norman Vincent Peale

The price if freedom is eternal vigilance.

Thomas Jefferson

A true leader has the confidence to stand alone, the courage to make tough decisions, and the compassion to listen to the needs of others. He does not set out to be a leader, but becomes one by the equality of his actions and the integrity of his intent.

Douglas McArthur

The real secret of success is enthusiasm.

Walter Chrysler

The condition of the most passionate enthusiast is to be preferred over the individual who, because of the fear of making a mistake, won't in the end affirm or deny anything.

**Thomas Carlyle**

Enthusiasm moves the world.

**Arthur James Balfour**

If you have zest and enthusiasm you attract zest and enthusiasm. Life does give back in kind.

**Norman Vincent Peale**

I prefer the folly of enthusiasm to the indifference of wisdom.

**Anatole France**

Catch on fire with enthusiasm and people will come for miles to watch you burn.

**John Wesley**

None are so old as those who have outlived enthusiasm.

**Henry David Thoreau**

A salesman minus enthusiasm is just a clerk.

**Harry F. Banks**

One man has enthusiasm for 30 minutes, another for 30 days, but it is the man who has it for 30 years who makes a success of his life.

**Edward B. Butler**

People rarely succeed unless they have fun in what they are doing.

**Dale Carnegie**

The love of life is necessary to the vigorous prosecution of any undertaking.

**Samuel Johnson**

No man who is enthusiastic about his work has anything to fear from life.

**Samuel Goldwyn**

If you are not getting as much from life as you want to, then examine the state of your enthusiasm.

**Norman Vincent Peale**

Do not be afraid of enthusiasm. You need it. You can do nothing effectively without it.

**Francois Pierre Guillaume Guizot**

Act enthusiastic and you become enthusiastic.

**Dale Carnegie**

What I do best is share my enthusiasm.

**Bill Gates**

There is a real magic in enthusiasm. It spells the difference between mediocrity and accomplishment.

**Norman Vincent Peale**

Do not quench your inspiration and your imagination; do not become the slave of your model.

**Vincent Van Gogh**

Goals provide the energy source that powers our lives. One of the best ways we can get the most from the energy we have is to focus it. That is what goals can do for us; concentrate our energy.

**Denis Waitley**

Enthusiasm is a vital element toward the individual success of every man or woman.

**Conrad Hilton**

If people around you aren't going anywhere, if their dreams are no bigger than hanging out on the corner, or if they're dragging you down, get rid of them. Negative people can sap your energy so fast, and they can take your dreams from you, too.

**Earvin "Magic" Johnson**

Our energy is in proportion to the resistance it meets.

**William Hazlitt**

Thoughts create a new heaven, a new firmament, a new source of energy, from which new arts flow.

**Philipus Aureolus Paracelsus**

Too many of us are hung up on what we don't have, can't have, or won't ever have. We spend too much energy being down, when we could use that same energy - if not less of it - doing, or at least trying to do, some of the things we really want to do.

**Terry McMillan**

You can have anything you want if you want it desperately enough. You must want it with an inner exuberance that erupts through the skin and joins the energy that created the world.

**Sheilah Graham**

And what is a man without energy? Nothing - nothing at all.

**Mark Twain**

Age is only a number, a cipher for the records. A man can't retire his experience. He must use it. Experience achieves more with less energy and time.

**Bernard Baruch**

Love the moment and the energy of the moment will spread beyond all boundaries.

**Sister Corita Kent**

---

# Chapter 14

A strong, successful man is not the victim of his environment. He creates favorable conditions. His own inherent force and energy compel things to turn out as he desires.

**Orison Swett Marden**

One essential to success is that your desire be an all-obsessing one, your thoughts and aim be coordinated, and your energy be concentrated and applied without letup.

**Claude M. Bristol**

Do you remember the things you were worrying about a year ago? How did they work out? Didn't you waste a lot of fruitless energy on account of most of them? Didn't most of them turn out all right after all?

**Dale Carnegie**

It takes as much energy to wish as it does to plan.

**Eleanor Roosevelt**

For purposes of action nothing is more useful than narrowness of thought combined with energy of will.

**Henri Frederic Amiel**

Most people spend more time and energy going around problems than in trying to solve them.

**Henry Ford**

It takes a lot more energy to fail than to succeed, since it takes a lot of concentrated energy to hold on to beliefs that don't work.

**Jerry Gillies**

The energy of the mind is the essence of life.

**Aristotle**

The higher your energy level, the more efficient your body. The more efficient your body, the better you feel and the more you will use your talent to produce outstanding results.

**Anthony Robbins**

A leader has the vision and conviction that a dream can be achieved. He inspires the power and energy to get it done.

**Ralph Lauren**

A person of intellect without energy added to it, is a failure.

**Sebastien-Roch Nicolas De Chamfort**

Energy and persistence alter all things.

**Benjamin Franklin**

If your energy is as boundless as your ambition, total commitment may be a way of life you should seriously consider.

**Dr. Joyce Brothers**

Energy is an eternal delight, and he who desires, but acts not, breeds pestilence.

**William Blake**

When you are in the valley, keep your goal firmly in view and you will get the renewed energy to continue the climb.

**Denis Waitley**

The more you lose yourself in something bigger than yourself, the more energy you will have.

**Norman Vincent Peale**

Flatter me, and I may not believe you. Criticize me, and I may not like you. Ignore me, and I may not forgive you. Encourage me, and I may not forget you

**William Arthur**

How far that little candle throws its beams! So shines a good deed in a naughty world.

**William Shakespeare (1564-1616) English Playwright**

Americanism means the virtues of courage, honor, justice, truth, sincerity, and hardihood the virtues that made America.

**Theodore Roosevelt (1858-1919) 26th President**

The more virtuous any man is, the less easily does he suspect others to be vicious.

**Marcus Tullius Cicero (106-43 BC)**
**Roman Writer, Statesman, and Orator**

It is a great mistake to think of being great without goodness; and I pronounce it as certain that there was never yet a truly great man that was not at the same time truly virtuous.

**Benjamin Franklin (1706-1790) American Statesman and Scientist**

In every person who comes near you look for what is good and strong; honor that; try to imitate it, and your faults will drop off like dead leaves when their time comes.

**John Ruskin (1819-1900) English Art Critic**

Man is so made that whenever anything fires his soul, impossibilities vanish.

**Jean de la Fontaine**

If a man hasn't discovered something that he would die for, he isn't fit to live.

**Martin Luther King, Jr. (1929-1968) American Civil Rights Leader**

Maturity is achieved when a person postpones immediate pleasures for long-term values.

**Joshua L. Liebman**

He who reigns within himself and rules his passions, desires, and fears is more than a king.

**John Milton (1608-1674) English Poet**

Honour, worthily obtained, is in its nature a personal thing, and incommunicable to any but those who had some share in obtaining it.

**Benjamin Franklin (1706-1790)**

From long familiarity, we know what honor is. It is what enables the individual to do right in the face of complacency and cowardice. It is what enables the soldier to die alone, the political prisoner to resist, the singer to sing her song, hardly appreciated, on a side street.

**Mark Helprin - American Novelist and Writer**

An army of sheep led by a lion would defeat an army of lions led by a sheep.

**Arab proverb**

I praise loudly; I blame softly.

**Catherine the Second (1729-1796) Russian Empress**

What you do speaks so loudly that I cannot hear what you say.

**Ralph Waldo Emerson (1803-1882) American Poet and Essayist**

Hold yourself responsible for a higher standard than anybody else expects of you. Never excuse yourself. Never pity yourself. Be a hard master to yourself - and be lenient to everybody else.

**Henry Ward Beecher (1813-1887) American Presbyterian Minister**

You can preach a better sermon with your life than with your lips.

**Oliver Goldsmith (1728-1774) Irish Writer**

I had rather do and not promise than promise and not do.

**Arthur Warwick**

The mediocre teacher tells. The good teacher explains. The superior teacher demonstrates. The great teacher inspires.

**William Arthur Ward**

Be the change that you want to see in the world.

**Mohandas Karamchand Gandhi (1869-1948) Indian Nationalist**

My basic principle is that you don't make decisions because they are cheap; you make them because they're right.

**Theodore Hesburgh (1917-) American, Former President of Notre Dame University**

When someone does something good, applaud! You will make two people happy.

**Samuel Goldwyn**

Children need models rather than critics.

**Joseph Joubert (1754-1824) French Philosopher**

We can often do more for other men by trying to correct our own faults than by trying to correct theirs.

**Francois Fenelon (1651-1715) French Roman Catholic Theologian**

I agree with you that there is a natural aristocracy among men. The grounds of this are virtue and talent.

**- from a letter to John Adams, 1813 Thomas Jefferson (1743-1826)**

One that desires to excel should endeavor in those things that are in themselves most excellent.

**Epictetus**

Achievement is not always success while reputed failure often is. It is honest endeavor, persistent effort to do the best possible under any and all circumstances.

**Orison Swett Marden**

Failures are finger posts on the road to achievement.

**Charles F. Kettering**

Let us, then, be up and doing, with a heart for any fate; still achieving, still pursuing, learn to labor and to wait.

**Henry Wadsworth Longfellow**

An achievement is a bondage. It obliges one to a higher achievement.

**Albert Camus**

Life is to be lived. If you have to support yourself, you had bloody well better find some way that is going to be interesting.

**Katharine Hepburn**

You can't build a reputation on what you're going to do.

**Henry Ford**

The way to get started is to quit talking and begin doing.

**Walt Disney**

What you get by achieving your goals is not as important as what you become by achieving your goals.

**Zig Ziglar**

One can never consent to creep when one feels an impulse to soar.

**Helen Keller**

To aim at the best and to remain essentially ourselves is one and the same thing.

**Janet Erskine Stuart**

An investment in knowledge always pays the best interest.

**Benjamin Franklin**

Only those who dare to fail greatly, can ever achieve greatly.

**Robert Kennedy**

The world of achievement has always belonged to the optimist.

**Harold Wilkins**

If we don't change, we don't grow If we don't grow, we aren't really living.

**Gail Sheehy**

Don't accept that others know you better than yourself. Work joyfully and peacefully, knowing that right thoughts and right efforts will inevitably bring about right results.

**James Allen**

Never mistake activity for achievement.

**John Wooden**

Achievement is largely the product of steadily raising one's levels of aspiration ... and expectation.

**Jack Nicklaus**

Nothing great will ever be achieved without great men, and men are great only if they are determined to be so.

**Charles De Gaulle**

There is more to life than increasing its speed.

**Gandhi**

Look at a day when you are supremely satisfied at the end. It's not a day when you lounge around doing nothing; it's when you've had everything to do, and you've done it.

**Margaret Thatcher**

Happiness...it lies in the joy of achievement, in the thrill of creative effort.

**Franklin D. Roosevelt**

The reason why worry kills more people than work is that more people worry than work.

**Robert Frost**

A wise man sees as much as he ought, not as much as he can.

**Montaigne**

If you fear making anyone mad, then you ultimately probe for the lowest common denominator of human achievement.

**Jimmy Carter**

For the things we have to learn before we can do them, we learn by doing them.

**Aristotle**

The secret of getting ahead is getting started.

**Sally Berger**

Presence is more than just being there.

**Malcolm S. Forbes**

Don't wait for someone to take you under their wing. Find a good wing and climb up underneath it.

**Frank C. Bucaro**

It is common sense to take a method and try it. If it fails, admit it frankly and try another. But above all, try something.

**Franklin D. Roosevelt**

The time for action is now. It's never too late to do something.

**Carl Sandburg**

---

It is the nature of thought to find its way into action.

**Christian Nevell Bovee**

Action springs not from thought, but from a readiness for responsibility.

**Dietrich Bonhoeffer**

Take action every day - some small dose at a time.

**Jeffrey Gitomer**

I think there is something, more important than believing: Action! The world is full of dreamers, there aren't enough who will move ahead and begin to take concrete steps to actualize their vision.

**W. Clement Stone**

Go for it now. The future is promised to no one.

**Wayne Dyer**

Begin doing what you want to do now. We have only this moment, sparkling like a star in our hand - and melting like a snowflake.

**Marie Beyon Ray**

As life is action and passion, it is required of a man that he should share the passion and action of his time, at the peril of being not to have lived.

**Oliver Wendell Holmes**

The best way you can predict your future is to create it.

**Stephen Covey**

This is the blessing of humankind, what separates us from the animals: to dream.

**Hugh Hefner**

When I examine myself and my methods of thought, I come to the conclusion that the gift of fantasy has meant more to me than my talent for absorbing positive knowledge.

**Albert Einstein (1879-1955) German-American Physicist**

At first dreams seem impossible, then improbable, then inevitable.

**Christopher Reeve (1952-) American Actor**

What is now proved was once only imagined.

**William Blake (1757-1827) English Poet**

My parents taught me that I could do anything I wanted and I have always believed it to be true. Add a clear idea of what inspires you, dedicate your energies to its pursuit and there is no knowing what you can achieve, particularly if others are inspired by your dream and offer their help.

**(from his book 'Close to the Wind'. Goss successfully sailed around the world - alone.) Pete Goss (1961-) British Sailor and Entrepreneur**

Far away in the sunshine are my highest aspirations. I may not reach them, but I can look up and see the beauty, believe in them and try to follow where they lead.

**Louisa May Alcott (1832-1888) American Writer**

All big things in this world are done by people who are naive and have an idea that is obviously impossible.

**Dr. Frank Richards (1875-1961) English Writer**

Mama exhorted her children at every opportunity to "jump at the Sun." We might not land on the sun, but at least we would get off the ground.

**Zora Neale Hurston (1903-1960) American Writer**

Far away in the sunshine are my highest aspirations. I may not reach them, but I can look up and see the beauty, believe in them and try to follow where they lead.

**Louisa May Alcott (1832-1888) American Writer**

The way to happiness: keep your heart free from hate, your mind from worry. Live simply, expect little, give much. Fill your life with love. Scatter sunshine. Forget self, think of others. Do as you would be done by. Try this for a week and you will be surprised.

**Norman Vincent Peale**

Happy are those who dream dreams and are ready to pay the price to make them come true.

**Leo Jozef Cardinal Suenens (1904-1996) Belgian Archbishop**

The young do not know enough to be prudent, and therefore they attempt the impossible -- and achieve it, generation after generation.

**Pearl S. Buck (1892-1973) American Writer**

If one advances confidently in the direction of his dreams, and endeavors to live a life which he has imagined, he will meet with a success unexpected in common hours.

**Henry David Thoreau (1817-1862)**
**American Philosopher and Writer**

Who would have ever heard of Theodore Roosevelt outside of his immediate community if he had only half committed himself to what he had undertaken, if he had brought only a part of himself to his task? The great secret of his career has been that he has flung his whole life, not a part of it, with all the determination and energy and power he could muster, into everything he has undertaken. No dillydallying, no faint-hearted efforts, no lukewarm purpose for him!

**Orison Swett Marden (1850-1924) American Editor and Speaker**

Cherish your visions and your dreams as they are the children of your soul; the blue prints of your ultimate accomplishments.

**Napoleon Hill (1883-1970) American Motivational Speaker**

Ah, but a man's reach should exceed his grasp, Or what's a heaven for?

**Robert Browning**

Aim at the sun and you may not reach it; but your arrow will fly far higher than if you had aimed at an object on a level with yourself.

**F. Hawes**

We act as though comfort and luxury were the chief requirements of life, when all that we need to make us really happy is something to be enthusiastic about.

**Charles Kingsley (1819-1875) English Novelist and Clergyman**

To say yes, you have to sweat and roll up your sleeves and plunge both hands into life up to the elbows.

**Jean Anouilh**

When we accept tough jobs as a challenge to our ability and wade into them with joy and enthusiasm, miracles can happen.

**Arland Gilbert**

When enthusiasm is inspired by reason, controlled by caution, sound in theory, practical in application, reflects confidence, spreads good cheer, raises morale, inspires associates, arouses loyalty, and laughs at adversity, it is beyond price.

**Coleman Cox**

Flaming enthusiasm, backed up by horse sense and persistence, is the quality that most frequently makes for success.

**Dale Carnegie (1888-1955) American Author and Speaker**

Nothing is so contagious as enthusiasm. It is the real allegory of the tale of Orpheus; it moves stones and charms brutes. It is the genius of sincerity and truth accomplishes no victories without it.

**Edward George Earle Bulwer-Lytton (1803-1873)**
**British Novelist and Politician**

Enthusiasm is the best protection in any situation. Wholeheartedness is contagious. Give yourself, if you wish to get others.

**David Seabury**

The vision that you glorify in your mind, the ideal that you enthrone in your heart - this you will build your life by, and this you will become.

**James Lane Allen (1849-1925)**
**American Author**

To live in the presence of great truths and eternal laws, to be led by permanent ideals - that is what keeps a man patient when the world ignores him, and calm and unspoiled when the world praises him.

**Honore De Balzac (1799-1850) French Novelist**

Enthusiasm glows, radiates, permeates and immediately captures everyone's interest.

**Paul J. Meyer**

The mind, ever the willing servant, will respond to boldness, for boldness, in effect, is a command to deliver mental resources.

**Author: Norman Vincent Peale**

If you want happiness for a lifetime help the next generation.

**Chinese proverb**

Nothing great was ever achieved without enthusiasm.

**Ralph Waldo Emerson**

What lies behind us and what lies before us are tiny matters compared to what lies within us.

**Ralph Waldo Emerson**

Everything has its wonders, even darkness and silence, and I learn, whatever state I may be in, therein to be content.

**Helen Keller**

For neither birth, nor wealth, nor honors, can awaken in the minds of men the principles which should guide those who from their youth aspire to an honorable and excellent life, as Love awakens them.

**Plato**

Knowledge is the food of the soul.

**Plato**

The man who makes everything that leads to happiness depend upon himself, and not upon other men, has adopted the very best plan for living happily.

**Plato**

...a friend ought always to do good to a friend and never evil.

**Plato**

...Love is that divinity who creates peace among men, repose and sleep in sadness. Love divests us of all alienation from each other, and fills our vacant hearts with overflowing sympathy...

**Plato**

Perseverance is a great element of success; if you only knock long enough and loud enough at the gate you are sure to wake up somebody.

**Henry Wadsworth Longfellow**

We judge ourselves by what we feel capable of doing, while others judge us by what we have already done.

**Henry Wadsworth Longfellow**

The heights by great men reached and kept were not attained by sudden flight, But they, while their companions slept, were toiling upward in the night.

**Henry Wadsworth Longfellow**

It takes less time to do a thing right than it does to explain why you did it wrong.

**Henry Wadsworth Longfellow**

Perseverance is a great element of success; if you only knock long enough and loud enough at the gate you are sure to wake up somebody.

**Henry Wadsworth Longfellow**

We shall neither fail nor falter; we shall not weaken or tire...Give us the tools and we will finish the job.

**Winston Churchill**

Never give in, never give in, never, never, never, never--in nothing, great or small, large or petty--never give in except to convictions of honor and good sense.

**Winston Churchill**

For myself, I am an optimist--it does not seem to be much use being anything else.

**Winston Churchill**

The only guide to man is his conscience; the only shield to his memory is the rectitude and sincerity of his actions. It is very imprudent to walk through life without this shield, because we are so often mocked by the failure of our hopes and the upsetting of our calculations; but with this shield, however the fates may play, we march always in the ranks of honor.

**Winston Churchill**

The empires of the future are the empires of the mind.

**Winston Churchill**

It is always wise to look ahead, but difficult to look farther than you can see.

**Winston Churchill**

If one has to submit, it is wasteful not to do so with the best grace possible.

**Winston Churchill**

All the great things are simple, and many can be expressed in a single word: freedom; justice; honor; duty; mercy; hope.

**Winston Churchill**

If we open a quarrel between the past and the present, we shall find we have lost the future.

**Winston Churchill**

Success is going from failure to failure without losing your enthusiasm.

**Winston Churchill**

One ought never to turn one's back on a threatened danger and try to run away from it. If you do that, you will double the danger. But if you meet it promptly and without flinching, you will reduce the danger by half. Never run away from anything. Never!

**Winston Churchill**

# Chapter 15

Courage is the first of the human qualities because it is the quality which guarantees all the others.

**Winston Churchill**

We shall draw from the heart of suffering itself the means of inspiration and survival.

**Winston Churchill**

Continuous effort--not strength or intelligence--is the key to unlocking our potential.

**Winston Churchill**

I never worry about action, but only about inaction.

**Winston Churchill**

A man is about as big as the things that make him angry.

**Winston Churchill**

There is nothing wrong with change, if it is in the right direction.

**Winston Churchill**

Courage is what it takes to stand up and speak; courage is also what it takes to sit down and listen.

**Winston Churchill**

It's not enough that we do our best; sometimes we have to do what's required.

**Winston Churchill**

We make a living by what we get, we make a life by what we give.

**Winston Churchill**

The price of greatness is responsibility.

**Winston Churchill**

An optimist sees an opportunity in every calamity; a pessimist sees a calamity in every opportunity.

**Winston Churchill**

If you mean to profit, learn to please.

**Winston Churchill**

It is better to do the wrong thing than to do nothing.

**Winston Churchill**

It helps to write down half a dozen things which are worrying me. Two of them, say, disappear; about two nothing can be done, so it's no use worrying; and two perhaps can be settled.

**Winston Churchill**

What is the use of living if it be not to strive for noble causes and to make this muddled world a better place for those who will live in it after we are gone.

**Winston Churchill**

Those who are not looking for happiness are the most likely to find it, because those who are searching forget that the surest way to be happy is to seek happiness for others."

**Martin Luthur King, Jr.**

One only gets to the top rung on the ladder by steadily climbing up one at a time, and suddenly, all sorts of powers, all sorts of abilities which you thought never belonged to you--suddenly become within your own possibility and you think, "Well, I'll have a go, too.

**Margaret Thatcher**

It is not the creation of wealth that is wrong, but the love of money for its own sake.

**Margaret Thatcher**

Standing in the middle of the road is very dangerous; you get knocked down by the traffic from both sides.

**Margaret Thatcher**

Everything you want in life has a price connected to it. There's a price to pay if you want to make things better, a price to pay just for leaving things as they are, a price for everything.

**Harry Browne**

The difference between perseverance and obstinacy is that one comes from a strong will, and the other from a strong won't.

**Henry Ward Beecher**

Beware of endeavoring to become a great man in a hurry. One such attempt in ten thousand may succeed. These are fearful odds.

**Benjamin Disraeli**

If it turns out that my best wasn't good enough, at least I won't look back and say that I was afraid to try; failure makes me work even harder.

**Michael Jordan**

Never explain - your friends do not need it and your enemies will not believe you anyway.

**Elbert Hubbard**

There would be nothing to frighten you if you refused to be afraid.

**Gandhi**

Class is an aura of confidence that is being sure without being cocky. Class has nothing to do with money. Class never runs scared. It is self-discipline and self-knowledge. It's the sure footedness that comes with having proved you can meet life.

**Ann Landers**

Outstanding leaders go out of their way to boost the self-esteem of their personnel. If people believe in themselves, it's amazing what they can accomplish.

**Sam Walton**

You cannot be lonely if you like the person you're alone with.

**Dr. Wayne W. Dyer**

Whatever good things we build end up building us.

**Jim Rohn**

Low self-esteem is like driving through life with your hand-break on.

**Maxwell Maltz**

You are indebted to you imagination for three-fourths of your importance.

**David Garrick**

Too many people overvalue what they are not and undervalue what they are.

**Malcolm S. Forbes**

Whatever games are played with us, we must play no games with ourselves.

**Ralph Waldo Emerson**

Let every man be respected as an individual and no man idolized.

**Albert Einstein**

He who stops being better stops being good.

**Oliver Cromwell**

Become addicted to constant and never ending self improvement.

**Anthony J. D'Angelo**

I don't think much of a man who is not wiser today than he was yesterday.

**Abraham Lincoln**

You can't have a better tomorrow if you are thinking about yesterday all the time.

**Charles F. Kettering**

The art of living lies less in eliminating our troubles than in growing with them.

**Bernard M. Baruch**

People seldom improve when they have no other model but themselves to copy after.

**Oliver Goldsmith**

It is necessary to try to surpass oneself always; this occupation ought to last as long as life.

**Christina {Queen of Sweden}**

Nurture your mind with great thoughts, for you will never go any higher than you think.

**Benjamin Disraeli**

People are like stained glass windows. They sparkle and shine when the sun is out, but when the darkness sets in, their true beauty is revealed only if there is a light from within.

**Elizabeth Kubler Ross**

Our scientific power has outrun our spiritual power. We have guided missiles and misguided men.

**Martin Luther King, Jr.**

You find that you have peace of mind and can enjoy yourself, get more sleep, rest when you know that it was a one hundred percent effort that you gave - win or lose.

**Gordie Howe**

I've always made a total effort, even when the odds seemed entirely against me. I never quit trying; I never felt that I didn't have a chance to win.

**Arnold Palmer**

Luck? Sure. But only after long practice and only with the ability to think under pressure.

**Babe Didrikson Zaharias**

Never let your head hang down. Never give up and sit down and grieve. Find another way. And don't pray when it rains if you don't pray when the sun shines.

**Leroy "Satchel" Paige**

The principle is competing against yourself. It's about self improvement, about being better than you were the day before.

**Steve Young**

One man can be a crucial ingredient on a team, but one man cannot make a team.

**Kareem Abdul-Jabbar**

My mother taught me very early to believe I could achieve any accomplishment I wanted to. The first was to walk without braces.

**Wilma Rudolph**

---

You can't live a perfect day without doing something for someone who will never be able to repay you.

**John Wooden**

The ideal attitude is to be physically loose and mentally tight.

**Arthur Ashe**

I've always believed that you can think positive just as well as you can think negative.

**Sugar Ray Robinson**

One man practicing sportsmanship is far better than 50 preaching it.

**Knute Rockne**

Doctors and scientists said that breaking the four-minute mile was impossible, that one would die in the attempt. Thus, when I got up from the track after collapsing at the finish line, I figured I was dead.

**Roger Bannister**

In order to excel, you must be completely dedicated to your chosen sport. You must also be prepared to work hard and be willing to accept constructive criticism. Without a total 100 percent dedication, you won't be able to do this.

**Willie Mays**

Treat a person as he is, and he will remain as he is. Treat him as he could be, and he will become what he should be.

**Jimmy Johnson**

I've always believed not matter how many shots I miss, I'm going to make the next one.

**Isiah Thomas**

Never let the fear of striking out get in your way.

**Babe Ruth**

Experience tells you what to do; confidence allows you to do it.

**Stan Smith**

You can't get much done in life if you only work on the days when you feel good.

**Jerry West**

I didn't just jump back on the bike and win. There were a lot of ups and downs, good results and bad results, but this time I didn't let the lows get to me.

**Lance Armstrong**

The secret to managing is to keep the guys who hate you away from the guys who are undecided.

**Casey Stengel**

It's what you learn after you know it all the counts.

**John Wooden**

I've failed over and over again in my life and that is why I succeed.

**Michael Jordan**

Paralyze resistance with persistence.

**Woody Hayes**

Show me someone who has done something worthwhile, and I'll show you someone who has overcome adversity.

**Lou Holtz**

You learn you can do your best when it's hard, even when you're tired and maybe hurting a little bit. It feels good to show some courage.

**Joe Namath**

Sports are 90% inspiration and 10% perspiration.

**Johnny Miller**

Champions aren't made in the gyms. Champions are made from something they have deep inside them: A desire, a dream, a vision.

**Muhammed Ali**

If you wait, all that happens is that you get older.

**Mario Andretti**

Sweat plus sacrifice equals success.

**Charles O. Finley**

Never give up, never give in, and when the upper hand is ours, may we have the ability to handle the win with the dignity that we absorbed the loss.

**Doug Williams**

A trophy carries dust. Memories last forever.

**Mary Lou Retton**

You may have to fight a battle more than once to win.

**Author: Margaret Thatcher**

If you just set out to be liked, you would be prepared to compromise on anything at any time, and you would achieve nothing.

**Margaret Thatcher**

Because your own strength is unequal to the task, do not assume that it is beyond the powers of man; but if anything is within the powers and province of man, believe that it is within your own compass also.

**Marcus Aurelius**

Very little is needed to make a happy life. It is all within yourself, in your way of thinking.

**Marcus Aurelius**

If you are distressed by anything external, the pain is not due to the thing itself but to your own estimate of it; and this you have the power to revoke at any moment.

**Marcus Aurelius**

The happiness of your life depends on the quality of your thoughts: therefore, guard accordingly, and take care that you entertain no notions unsuitable to virtue and reasonable nature.

**Marcus Aurelius**

Execute every act of thy life as though it were thy last.

**Marcus Aurelius**

A man's worth is no greater than the worth of his ambitions.

**Marcus Aurelius Antoninus**

Consider how much more you often suffer from your anger and grief, than from those very things for which you are angry and grieved.

**Marcus Aurelius Antoninus**

To do is to be.

**Socrates**

False words are not only evil in themselves, but they infect the soul with evil.

**Socrates**

Better to do a little well, then a great deal badly.

**Socrates**

Loneliness is the most terrible poverty.

**Mother Teresa**

The ocean is made of drops.

**Mother Teresa**

---

Your own soul is nourished when you are kind; it is destroyed when you are cruel.

**King Solomon**

Where there is no vision, the people perish.

**King Solomon**

People become really quite remarkable when they start thinking that they can do things. When they believe in themselves they have the first secret of success.

**Norman Vincent Peale**

Never talk defeat. Use words like hope, belief, faith, victory.

**Norman Vincent Peale**

Joy increases as you give it, and diminishes as you try to keep it for yourself. In giving it, you will accumulate a deposit of joy greater than you ever believed possible.

**Norman Vincent Peale**

Live your life and forget your age.

**Norman Vincent Peale**

Those who are fired with an enthusiastic idea and who allow it to take hold and dominate their thoughts find that new worlds open for them. As long as enthusiasm holds out, so will new opportunities.

**Norman Vincent Peale**

Practice hope. As hopefulness becomes a habit, you can achieve a permanently happy spirit.

**Norman Vincent Peale**

If you want to get somewhere you have to know where you want to go and how to get there. Then never, never, never give up.

**Norman Vincent Peale**

Men are born with two eyes, but only one tongue, in order that they should see twice as much as they say.

**Charles Caleb Colton**

It seemed rather incongruous that in a society of super sophisticated communication, we often suffer from a shortage of listeners.

**Erma Bombeck**

Speech is for the convenience of those who are hard of hearing; but there are many fine things which we cannot say if we have to shout.

**Henry David Thoreau**

I like to listen. I have learned a great deal from listening carefully. Most people never listen.

**Ernest Hemingway**

It's good to shut up sometimes.

**Marcel Marceau**

If there is any great secret of success in life, it lies in the ability to put yourself in the other person's place and to see things from his point of view – as well as your own.

**Henry Ford**

Do not say a little in many words but a great deal in a few.

**Pythagoras**

Words are, of course, the most powerful drug used by mankind.

**Rudyard Kipling**

The difference between the right word and the almost right word is the difference between lightning and a lightning bug.

**Mark Twain**

The only way to get the best of an argument is to avoid it.

**Dale Carnegie**

The ability to speak eloquently is not to be confused with having something to say.

**Michael P. Hart**

When your writing is filled with detail, it has a lot more impact.

**Ivan Levison**

First learn the meaning of what you say, and then speak.

**Epictetus**

One of the lessons of history is that nothing is often a good thing to do and always a clever thing to say.

**Will Durant**

If you have nothing to say, say nothing.

**Mark Twain**

Give me the gift of a listening heart.

**King Solomon**

Remember, what you say comes back to you.

**Zig Ziglar**

They may forget what you said, but they will never forget how you made them feel.

**Carl W. Buechner**

When dealing with people, remember you are not dealing with creatures of logic, but creatures of emotion.

**Dale Carnegie**

Saying nothing...sometimes says the most.

**Emily Dickinson**

The most important things are the hardest to say, because words diminish them.

**Stephen King**

I don't let my mouth say nothin' my head can't stand.

**Louis Armstrong**

Who speads, sows; Who listens, reaps.

**Argentine Proverb**

If speaking is silver, then listening is gold.

**Turkish Proverb**

Speak when you are angry and you will make the best speech you will ever regret.

**Ambrose Bierce**

Say what you mean and mean what you say.

**George S. Patton**

You cannot truly listen to anyone and do anything else at the same time.

**M. Scott Peck**

Be amusing: never tell unkind stories; above all, never tell long ones.

**Benjamin Disraeli**

Speak clearly, if you speak at all; carve every word before you let it fall.

**Oliver Wendell Holmes**

---

I remind myself every morning: Nothing I say this day will teach me anything. So if I'm going to learn, I must do it by listening.

**Larry King**

One learns people through the heart, not the eyes or the intellect.

**Mark Twain**

The greatest compliment that was ever paid me was when one asked me what I thought, and attended to my answer.

**Henry David Thoreau**

Big egos have little ears.

**Robert Schuller**

You can have brilliant ideas, but if you can't get them across, your ideas won't get you anywhere.

**Lee Iacocca**

The ear of the leader must ring with the voices of the people.

**Woodrow Wilson**

The key to success is to get out into the store and listen to what the associates have to say. It's terribly important for everyone to get involved. Our best ideas come from clerks and stockboys.

**Sam Walton**

Listening, not imitation, may be the sincerest form of flattery.

**Dr. Joyce Brothers**

Drop the idea that you are Atlas carrying the world on your shoulders. The world would go on even without you. Don't take yourself so seriously.

**Norman Vincent Peale**

The "how" thinker gets problems solved effectively because he wastes no time with futile "ifs" but goes right to work on the creative "how."

**Norman Vincent Peale**

Resentment or grudges do no harm to the person against whom you hold these feelings but every day and every night of your life, they are eating at you.

**Norman Vincent Peale**

When a problem comes along, study it until you are completely knowledgeable. Then find that weak spot, break the problem apart, and the rest will be easy.

**Norman Vincent Peale**

Enthusiasm releases the drive to carry you over obstacles and adds significance to all you do.

**Norman Vincent Peale**

It's always too soon to quit!

**Norman Vincent Peale**

Our happiness depends on the habit of mind we cultivate. So practice happy thinking every day. Cultivate the merry heart, develop the happiness habit, and life will become a continual feast.

**Norman Vincent Peale**

Life's blows cannot break a person whose spirit is warmed at the fire of enthusiasm.

**Norman Vincent Peale**

You can be greater than anything that can happen to you.

**Norman Vincent Peale**

One way to become enthusiastic is to look for the plus sign. To make progress in any difficult situation, you have to start with what's right about it and build on that.

**Norman Vincent Peale**

To go fast, row slowly.

**Norman Vincent Peale**

The "as if" principle works. Act "as if" you were not afraid and you will become courageous, "as if" you could and you'll find you can. Act "as if" you like a person and you'll find a friendship.

**Norman Vincent Peale**

Yesterday ended last night. Every day is a new beginning. Learn the skill of forgetting. And move on.

**Norman Vincent Peale**

The cyclone derives its powers from a calm center. So does a person.

**Norman Vincent Peale**

You are greater than you think you are.

**Norman Vincent Peale**

Problems are to the mind what exercise is to the muscles, they toughen and make strong.

**Norman Vincent Peale**

Every man has his own courage, and is betrayed because he seeks in himself the courage of other persons.

**Ralph Waldo Emerson**

Be humble, be big in mind and soul, be kindly; you will like yourself that way and so will other people.

**Norman Vincent Peale**

The way to happiness: keep your heart free from hate, your mind from worry. Live simply, expect little, give much. Fill your life with love. Scatter sunshine. Forget self, think of others. Do as you would be done by. Try this for a week and you will be surprised.

**Norman Vincent Peale**

Cut the "im" out of impossible, leading that dynamic word standing out free and clear -- possible.

**Norman Vincent Peale**

Never react emotionally to criticism. Analyze yourself to determine whether it is justified. If it is, correct yourself. Otherwise, go on about your business.

**Norman Vincent Peale**

How you think about a problem is more important than the problem itself -- so always think positively.

**Norman Vincent Peale**

# Chapter 16

When you are afraid, do the thing you are afraid of and soon you will lose your fear of it.

**Norman Vincent Peale**

If you want things to be different, perhaps the answer is to become different yourself.

**Norman Vincent Peale**

Remember, there is no situation so completely hopeless that something constructive cannot be done about it. When faced with a minus, ask yourself what you can do to make it a plus. A person practicing this attitude will extract undreamed-of outcomes from the most unpromising situations. Realize that there are no hopeless situations; there are only people who take hopeless attitudes.

**Norman Vincent Peale**

I never worry about the future. It comes soon enough.

**Albert Einstein**

There is only one road to true human greatness: through the school of hard knocks.

**Albert Einstein**

Imagination is more important than knowledge.

**Albert Einstein**

The value of achievement lies in the achieving.

**Albert Einstein**

Laughter is the shortest distance between two people.

**Victor Borge**

When inspiration does not come to me, I go halfway to meet it.

**Sigmund Freud**

Laughter is an instant vacation.

**Milton Berle**

The state of your life is nothing more than a reflection of your state of mind.

**Dr. Wayne W. Dyer**

Creativity means believing you have greatness.

**Dr. Wayne W. Dyer**

Your reputation is in the hands of others. That's what a reputation is. You can't control that. The only thing you can control is your character.

**Dr. Wayne W. Dyer**

The man who has no imagination has no wings.

**Muhammad Ali**

Age does not protect you from love. But love, to some extent, protects you from age.

**Jeanne Moreau, French Actress**

Far better is it to dare mighty things, to win glorious triumphs-even though checkered by failure than to take rank with these poor spirits who neither enjoy much or suffer much. Be wise, they live in the gray twilight that know not of victory, nor defeat. Nor true sorrow nor true love.

**Theodore Roosevelt**

Happiness lies in the joy of achievement and the thrill of creative effort.

**Franklin D. Roosevelt 32nd president of the United States**

Gentlemen, Why don't you laugh? With the fearful strain that is upon me night and day, if I did not laugh, I would die.

**Abraham Lincoln (1809-1865)**

Somehow I can't believe that there are any heights that can't be scaled by a man who knows the secrets of making dreams come true. This special secret, it seems to me, can be summarized in four C's. They are curiosity, confidence, courage, and constancy, and the greatest of all is confidence. When you believe in a thing, believe in it all the way, implicitly and unquestionable.

**Walt Disney**

Four freedoms: The first is freedom of speech and expression - everywhere in the world. The second is freedom of everyone to worship God in his own way, everywhere in the world. The third is freedom from want.... everywhere in the world. The fourth is freedom from fear... anywhere in the world.

**Franklin D. Roosevelt U.S. President**

Courage is the greatest of all virtues, because if you haven't courage, you may not have an opportunity to use any of the others.

**Samuel Johnson**

Don't be afraid of the space between your dreams and reality. If you can dream it, you can make it so.

**Belva Davis**

There are some people who live in a dream world, and there are some who face reality; and then there are those who turn one into the other.

**Douglas Everett**

Who, being loved, is poor?

**Oscar Wilde**

While there's life, there's hope!

**Ancient Roman Saying**

Hope is a waking dream.

**Aristotle (384-322 B.C.)**

Hope is necessary in every condition. The miseries of poverty, sickness and captivity would, without this comfort, be insupportable.

**Samuel Johnson**

We must accept finite disappointment, but we must never lose infinite hope.

**Dr. Martin Luther King Jr.**

Hope is not the conviction that something will turn out well, but the certainty that something makes sense regardless of how it turns out.

**Vaclav Havel**

Your hopes, dreams and aspirations are legitimate. They are trying to take you airborne, above the clouds, above the storms, if you only let them.

**William James**

We should not let our fears hold us back from pursuing our hopes.

**John F. Kennedy**

Every area of trouble gives out a ray of hope; and the one unchangeable certainty is that nothing is certain or unchangeable.

**John F. Kennedy**

People like you and I, though mortal of course like everyone else, do not grow old no matter how long we live...[We] never cease to stand like curious children before the great mystery into which we were born.

**Albert Einstein in a letter to Otto Juliusburger**

---

To fulfill a dream, to be allowed to sweat over lonely labor, to be given a chance to create, is the meat and potatoes of life. The money is the gravy.

**Bette Davis**

Stop the mindless wishing that things would be different. Rather than wasting time and emotional and spiritual energy in explaining why we don't have what we want, we can start to pursue other ways to get it.

**Greg Anderson US basketball player**

We grow great by dreams ... Some of us let these great dreams die, but others nourish and protect them; nurse them through bad days till they [flourish]; bring them to the sunshine and light, which comes always to those who sincerely hope that their dreams will come true.

**Woodrow Wilson**

Dreams are great. When they disappear you may still be here, but you will have ceased to live.

**Lady Nancy Astor**

Trust in dreams, for in them is the hidden gate to eternity.

**Kahill Gibran**

Don't be afraid of the space between your dreams and reality. If you can dream it, you can make it so.

**Belva Davis**

We grow great by dreams. All big men are dreamers. They see things in the soft haze of a spring day or in the red fire of a long winter's evening. Some of us let these great dreams die, but others nourish and protect them; nurse them through bad days till they bring them to the sunshine and light which comes always to those who sincerely hope that their dreams will come true.

**Woodrow Wilson, 28th US President**

There will always be dreams grander or humbler than your own, but there will never be a dream exactly like your own...for you are unique and more wondrous than you know!

**Linda Staten**

Dream as if you'll live forever... live as if you'll die today.

**James Dean**

I would rather be ashes than dust! I would rather that my spark should burn out in a brilliant blaze than it should be stifled by dry rot. I would rather be a superb meteor, every atom of me in magnificent glow, than a sleepy and permanent planet. The proper function of man is to live, not to exist. I shall not waste my days in trying to prolong them. I shall use my time.

**Jack London, American Author**

The future belongs to those who believe in the beauty of their dreams.

**Eleanor Roosevelt, American First Lady**

Some men see things as they are and ask why. Others dream things that never were and ask why not.

**George Bernard Shaw, Irish Playwright and Critic**

All men and women are born, live suffer and die; what distinguishes us one from another is our dreams, whether they be dreams about worldly or unworldly things, and what we do to make them come about... We do not choose to be born. We do not choose our parents. We do not choose our historical epoch, the country of our birth, or the immediate circumstances of our upbringing. We do not, most of us, choose to die; nor do we choose the time and conditions of our death. But within this realm of choicelessness, we do choose how we live.

**Joseph Epstein**

If you can dream it, you can do it.

**Walt Disney**

---

Dare to live the life you have dreamed for yourself. Go forward and make your dreams come true.

**Ralph Waldo Emerson**

It is difficult to say what is impossible, for the dream of yesterday is the hope of today and the reality of tomorrow.

**Robert H. Goddard**

Keep away from people who try to belittle your ambitions. Small people always do that, but the really great make you feel that you, too, can become great.

**Mark Twain**

Reach high, for stars lie hidden in your soul. Dream deep, for every dream precedes the goal.

**Pamela Vaull Starr**

Dreams are the touchstone of our character.

**Henry David Thoreau**

Those who lose dreaming are lost.

**Australian Aboriginal Proverb**

In your heart, keep one still secret spot where dreams may go and be sheltered so they may thrive and grow.

**Louise Driscoll**

All men who have achieved great things have been great dreamers.

**Orison Swett Marsden**

If one advances confidently in the direction of their dreams, and endeavors to lead a life which they have imagined, they will meet with a success unexpected in common hours.

**Henry David Thoreau**

---

A dream is an answer to a question we haven't yet learned how to ask.

**Fox Mulder**


Self-esteem must be earned! When you dare to dream, dare to follow that dream, dare to suffer through the pain, sacrifice, self-doubts, and friction from the world, you will genuinely impress yourself.

**Dr. Laura Schlessinger**


Whatever you are, be a good one.

**Abraham Lincoln (1809-1865)**


The best thing about the future is that it comes only one day at a time.

**Abraham Lincoln (1809-1865)**


Am I not destroying my enemies when I make friends of them?

**Abraham Lincoln**


Quarrel not at all. No man resolved to make the most of himself can spare time for personal contention. Still less can he afford to take all the consequences, including the vitiating of his temper and loss of self-control.

**Abraham Lincoln (1809-1865)**


Most people are about as happy as they make up their minds to be.

**Abraham Lincoln**


You have to do your own growing no matter how tall your grandfather was.

**Abraham Lincoln**


It has been my experience that folks who have no vices have very few virtues.

**Abraham Lincoln**

He will have to learn, I know, that all people are not just- that all men and women are not true. Teach him that for every scoundrel there is a hero that for every enemy there is a friend. Let him learn early that the bullies are the easiest people to lick.

**Abraham Lincoln**

Four score and seven years ago our fathers brought forth on this continent a new nation, conceived in liberty, and dedicated to the proposition that all men are created equal.

**Abraham Lincoln**

The best advice I can give is to ignore advice. Life is too short to be distracted by the opinions of others.

**Russel Edson**

I like living. I have sometimes been wildly, despairingly, acutely miserable, racked with sorrow, but through it all I still know quite certainly that just to be alive is a grand thing.

**Agatha Christie (1890 - 1976)**

Let us rise up and be thankful, for if we didn't learn a lot today, at least we learned a little, and if we didn't learn a little, at least we didn't get sick, and if we got sick, at least we didn't die; so, let us all be thankful.

**Buddha**

Courage is not the absence of fear, but rather the judgment that something else is more important than fear.

**Ambrose Redmoon**

With courage you will dare to take risks, have the strength to be compassionate and the wisdom to be humble. Courage is the foundation of integrity.

**Keshavan Nair**

Don't let the fear of the time it will take to accomplish something stand in the way of your doing it. The time will pass anyway; we might just as well put that passing time to the best possible use.

**Earl Nightingale**


People of mediocre ability sometimes achieve outstanding success because they don't know when to quit. Most men succeed because they are determined to.

**George H. Allen**


There are only two options regarding commitment. You're either IN or you're OUT. There is no such thing as life in-between.

**Pat Riley**


We are very near to greatness: one step and we are safe; can we not take the leap?

**Ralph Waldo Emerson**


Leaders are visionaries with a poorly developed sense of fear and no concept of the odds against them. They make the impossible happen.

**Dr. Robert Jarvik**


Determination gives you the resolve to keep going in spite of the roadblocks that lay before you.

**Denis Waitley**


There's nothing in this world that comes easy. There are a lot of people who aren't going to bother to win. We learn in football to get up and go once more.

**Woody Hayes**


If you don't invest very much, then defeat doesn't hurt very much and winning isn't very exciting.

**Dick Vermiel**

I couldn't wait for success, so I went ahead without it.

**Jonathan Winters**

The Key to immortality is to live a life worth remembering.

**Bruce Lee (1940-1973)**

Don't always follow the crowd, because nobody goes there anymore.

**Yogi Berra**

The winners in life think constantly in terms of I can, I will, and I am. Losers, on the other hand, concentrate their waking thoughts on what they should have or would have done, or what they can't do.

**Dennis Waitley**

Success in life has nothing to do with what you gain in life or accomplish for yourself. It's what you do for others.

**Danny Thomas**

Empty pockets never held anyone back. Only empty heads and empty hearts can do that.

**Norman Vincent Peale**

As long as you derive inner help and comfort from anything, keep it.

**Mahatma Gandhi (1869 - 1948)**

Life is like a game of cards. The hand that is dealt you is determinism; the way you play it is free will.

**Jawaharlal Nchru (1889 - 1964)**

Management is nothing more than motivating other people.

**Lee Iacocca (1924 - )**

A human being is only interesting if he's in contact with himself. I learned you have to trust yourself, be what you are, and do what you ought to do the way you should do it. You have got to discover you, what you do, and trust it.

**Barbra Streisand (1942 - )**

When the character of a man is not clear to you, look at his friends.

**Japanese Proverb**

I don't know the key to success, but the key to failure is trying to please everybody.

**Bill Cosby (1937 - )**

You can have everything in life you want if you'll just help enough other people to get what they want!

**Zig Ziglar**

Show class, have pride, and display character. If you do, winning takes care of itself.

**Coach Paul "Bear" Bryant**

Work like you don't need the money. Love like you've never been hurt. Dance like nobody is watching.

**Mark Twain / Samuel Clements**

Vision without action is a daydream. Action without vision is a nightmare.

**Japanese Proverb**

And in the end, it's not the years in your life that count. It's the life in your years.

**Abraham Lincoln**

All life is an experiment.

**Ralph Waldo Emerson**

---

Nothing great was ever achieved without enthusiasm.

**Ralph Waldo Emerson**

The only way to have a friend is to be one.

**Ralph Waldo Emerson**

We aim above the mark to hit the mark.

**Ralph Waldo Emerson**

One should guard against preaching to young people success in the customary form as the main aim in life. The most important motive for work in school and in life is pleasure in work, pleasure in its result, and the knowledge of the value of the result to the community.

**Albert Einstein**

Life is too short to be small.

**Benjamin Disraeli**

Hope is the companion of power, and mother of success; for who so hopes strongly has within him the gift of miracles.

**Samuel Smiles**

To educate yourself for the feeling of gratitude means to take nothing for granted, but to always seek out and value the kindness that stands behind the action. Nothing that is done for you is a matter of course. Everything originates in a will for the good, which is directed at you. Train yourself never to put off the word or action for the expression of gratitude.

**Albert Schweitzer**

The great French Marshall Lyautey once asked his gardener to plant a tree. The gardener objected that the tree was slow growing and would not reach maturity for 100 years. The Marshall replied, "In that case, there is no time to lose. Plant it this afternoon!

**John F. Kennedy**

Develop serenity and quiet attitudes through your conversation. Depending upon the words we use and the tone in which we use them, we can talk ourselves into being nervous, high-strung, and upset. By our speech, we can also achieve quiet reactions. Talk peaceful to be peaceful.

**Norman Vincent Peale**

The real glory is being knocked to your knees and then coming back. That's real glory. That's the essence of it.

**Vince Lombardi**

Fall seven times; stand up eight.

**Japanese Proverb**

When you get in a tight place and everything goes against you, till it seems as though you could not hold on a minute longer, never give up then, for that is just the place and time that the tide will turn.

**Harriet Beecher Stowe**

Let's cease thinking of our accomplishments, our wants. Let's try to figure out the other man's good points. Then forget flattery. Give honest, sincere appreciation. Be "hearty in your approbation and lavish in your praise," and people will cherish your words and treasure them and repeat them over a lifetime -- repeat them years after you have forgotten them.

**Dale Carnegie**

Success is never permanent, and failure is never final.

**Mike Ditka**

If I were asked to give what I consider the single most useful bit of advice for all humanity, it would be this: Expect trouble as an inevitable part of life, and when it comes, hold your head high. Look it squarely in the eye, and say, "I will be bigger than you. You cannot defeat me.

**Ann Landers**

I have had dreams and I have had nightmares, but I have conquered my nightmares because of my dreams.

**Dr. Jonas Salk**

We create our lives a thought at a time. And sometimes, it comes down to changing a thought such as "Why did this happen to me?" into "There is a divine plan and there is a reason for this, and my choice is to create the most positive reaction I can.

**Dee Wallace Stone**

If we want a free and peaceful world, if we want to make the deserts bloom and man grow to greater dignity as a human being -- we can do it.

**Eleanor Roosevelt**

If I have the belief that I can do it, I shall surely acquire the capacity to do it even if I may not have it at the beginning.

**Mahatma Gandhi**

Waste no tears over the griefs of yesterday.

**Euripides**

Never say anything to hurt anyone. Moreover... refrain from double talk, from shrewd and canny remarks that are designed to advance our interests at someone's disadvantage. We are to turn our back upon evil, and in every way possible, do good, help people and bring blessings into their lives.

**Norman Vincent Peale**

Great works are performed not by strength but by perseverance.

**Samuel Johnson**

Ability may get you to the top, but it takes character to keep you there.

**John Wooden**

Consult not your fears but your hopes and your dreams. Think not about your frustrations, but about your unfulfilled potential. Concern yourself not with what you tried and failed in, but with what it is still possible for you to do.

**Pope John XXIII**

Through perseverance many people win success out of what seemed destined to be certain failure.

**Benjamin Disraeli**

If opportunity doesn't knock build a door.

**Milton Berle**

You may be disappointed if you fail, but you are doomed if you don't try.

**Beverly Sills**

You can't always control the wind, but you can control your sails.

**Anthony Robbins**

It's never crowded along the extra mile.

**Dr. Wayne Dyer**

Excellence is to do a common thing in an uncommon way.

**Booker T. Washington**

I cannot always control what goes on outside. But I can always control what goes on inside.

**Wayne Dyer**

Life is a great big canvas and you should throw all the paint on it you can.

**Danny Kaye**

I plan on growing old much later in life, or maybe not at all.

**Patty Carey**

The harder you work, the luckier you get.

**Gary Player**

"Happiness"

# Chapter 17

We are all in the gutter but some of us are gazing at stars.

**Oscar Wilde**

A time comes when you need to stop waiting for the man you want to become and start being the man you want to be.

**Bruce Springsteen**

Whether you think you can or cannot you are usually right.

**Henry Ford**

You ask what our aim is. I can answer in one word - VICTORY. Victory at all costs, Victory in spite of fear, Victory, however long and hard the road may be.

**Winston Churchill**

Adopt the pace of nature, her secret is patience.

**Ralph Waldo Emerson**

You miss 100% of the shots you don't take.

**Wayne Gretzky**

Get excited and enthusiastic about your own dream. This excitement is like a forest fire -- you can smell it, taste it, and see it from a mile away.

**Denis Waitley**

Don't let yesterday use up too much of today.

**Will Rogers**

Half our life is spent trying to find something to do with the time we have rushed through life trying to save.

**Will Rogers**

Live in such a way that you would not be ashamed to sell you parrot to the town gossip.

**Will Rogers**

Every man's life ends the same way. It is only the details of how he lived and how he died that distinguish one man from another.

**Ernest Hemingway**

The more one does and sees and feels, the more one is able to do, and the more genuine may be one's appreciation of fundamental things like home, and love, and understanding companionship.

**Amelia Earhart**

The most effective way to do it, is to do it.

**Amelia Earhart**

The most difficult thing is the decision to act, the rest is merely tenacity. The fears are paper tigers. You can do anything you decide to do. You can act to change and control your life; and the procedure, the process is its own reward.

**Amelia Earhart**

Not knowing when the dawn will come, I open every door.

**Emily Dickinson**

Perseverance is the hard work you do after you get tired of doing the hard work you already did.

**Newt Gingrich**

Much good work is lost for the lack of a little more.

**Edward Harriman**

The greater the difficulty the more glory in surmounting it. Skillful pilots gain their reputation from storms and tempests.

**Epictetus**

If you want to get somewhere you have to know where you want to go and how to get there. Then never, never, never give up.

**Norman Vincent Peale**

It's not the load that breaks you down, it's the way you carry it.

**Lena Horne**

Great things are not done by impulse, but by a series of small things brought together.

**Vincent Van Gogh**

In the middle of difficulty lies opportunity.

**Albert Einstein**

The saints are the sinners who keep going.

**Robert Louis Stevenson**

Home run hitters strike out a lot.

**Reggie Jackson**

The reward of a thing well done is to have done it.

**Ralph Waldo Emerson**

Problems are to the mind what exercise is to the muscles, they toughen and make strong.

**Norman Vincent Peale**

I learned that the only way you are going to get anywhere in life is to work hard at it. Whether you're a musician, a writer, an athlete or a businessman, there is no getting around it. If you do, you'll win - if you don't you won't.

**Bruce Jenner**

Nothing in the world can take the place of persistence. Talent will not; nothing is more common than unsuccessful men with talent. Genius will not; unrewarded genius is almost a proverb. Education will not; the world is full of educated derelicts. Persistence and determination are omnipotent.

**Calvin Coolidge**

When you come to a roadblock, take a detour.

**Mary Kay Ash**

I have not failed. I've just found 10,000 ways that won't work.

**Thomas Edison**

The best way you can predict your future is to create it.

**Stephen Covey**

Be not afraid of growing slowly, be afraid only of standing still.

**Chinese Proverb**

A little knowledge that acts is worth infinitely more than much knowledge that is idle.

**Kahlil Gibran**

For purposes of action nothing is more useful than narrowness of thought combined with energy of will.

**Henri Frederic Amiel**

Either move or be moved.

**Colin Powell**

Action is the foundational key to all success.

**Anthony Robbins**

The few who do are the envy of the many who only watch.

**Jim Rohn**

You will never win if you never begin.

**Robert Schuller**

Heaven never helps the men who will not act.

**Sophocles**

The world cares very little about what a man or woman knows; it is what a man or woman is able to do that counts.

**Booker T. Washington**

People may doubt what you say, but they will believe what you do.

**Lewis Cass**

Begin to free yourself at once by doing all that is possible with the means you have, and as you proceed in this spirit the way will open for you to do more.

**Robert Collier**

You have to sow before you can reap. You have to give before you can get.

**Robert Collier**

Everyone who got where he is had to begin where he was.

**Richard L. Evans**

A man is the sum of his actions, of what he has done, of what he can do, Nothing else.

**Mahatma Gandhi**

The more we do, the more we can do; the more busy we are, the more leisure we have.
**William Hazlitt**

Our grand business in life is not to see what lies dimly at a distance, but to do what lies clearly at hand.

**Thomas Carlyle**

What we need is to use what we have.

**Basil S. Walsh**

Nobody made a greater mistake than he who did nothing because he could do only a little.

**Edmund Burke**

Be an all-out, not a hold-out.

**Norman Vincent Peale**

You must take action now that will move you towards your goals. Develop a sense of urgency in your life.

**Les Brown**

Everything you want is out there waiting for you to ask. Everything you want also wants you. But you have to take action to get it.

**Jack Canfield**

First say to yourself what you would be; and then do what you have to do.

**Epictetus**

All men of action are dreamers.

**James G. Huneker**

Iron rusts from disuse, stagnant water loses its purity, and in cold weather becomes frozen, even so does inaction sap the vigor of the mind.

**Leonardo Da Vinci**

The only way to discover the limits of the possible is to go beyond them into the impossible.

**Arthur C. Clarke**

Do not confuse motion and progress. A rocking horse keeps moving but does not make any progress.

**Alfred A. Montapert**

An ounce of action is worth a ton of theory.

**Friedrich Engels**

Don't be afraid your life will end; be afraid that it will never begin.

**Grace Hansen**

Doing is a quantum leap from imagining. Thinking about swimming isn't much like actually getting in the water.

**Barbara Sher**

Do not be too timid and squeamish about your actions. All life is an experiment.

**Ralph Waldo Emerson**

Deliberation is the work of many men. Action, of one alone.

**Charles De Gaulle**

Take time to deliberate; but when the time for action arrives, stop thinking and go in.

**Andrew Jackson**

Action may not bring happiness but there is no happiness without action.

**William James**

He who desires but acts not, breeds pestilence.

**William Blake**

---

As I grow older, I pay less attention to what men say. I just watch what they do.

**Andrew Carnegie**

Conditions are never just right. People who delay action until all factors are favorable do nothing.

**William Feather**

Without promotion, something terrible happens - nothing!

**P.T. Barnum**

Let him who would move the world, first move himself.

**Socrates**

Things won are done; joy's soul lies in the doing.

**William Shakespeare**

We always overestimate the change that will occur in the next two years and underestimate the change that will occur in the next ten. Don't let yourself be lulled into inaction.

**Bill Gates**

If doubt is challenging you and you do not act, doubts will grow. Challenge the doubts with action and you will grow. Doubt and action are incompatible.

**John Kanary**

To think is easy. To act is difficult. To act as one thinks is the most difficult.

**Johann Wolfgang Von Goeth**

An ounce of action is worth a ton of theory.

**Friedrich Engels**

If you want to know your past - look into your present conditions. If you want to know your future - look into your present actions.

**Chinese proverb**

Knowing is not enough; we must apply. Willing is not enough; we must do.

**Johann von Goethe**

Abundance is from activity.

**Turkish proverb**

If you want to accomplish anything in life, you can't just sit back and hope it will happen. You've got to make it happen.

**Chuck Norris**

Whatever you do may seem insignificant to you, but it is most important that you do it.

**Mahatma Gandhi**

It is time for us all to stand and cheer for the doer, the achiever - the one who recognizes the challenge and does something about it.

**Vincent Lombardi**

Small deeds done are better than great deeds planned.

**Peter Marshall**

If you can't sleep, then get up and do something instead of lying there worrying. It's the worry that gets you, not the lack of sleep.

**Dale Carnegie**

Genius is the ability to put into effect what is on your mind.

**F. Scott Fitzgerald**

Our deeds determine us, as much as we determine our deeds.

**George Eliot**

You must do the thing you think you cannot do.

**Eleanor Roosevelt**

I am a verb.

**Ulysses S. Grant**

Courage is dying what you're afraid to do. There can be no courage unless you're scared.

**Eddie Rickenbacker**

What may be done at any time will be done at no time.

**Scottish proverb**

The things you refuse to meet today always come back at you later on, usually under circumstances twice as difficult as it originally was.

**Eleanor Roosevelt**

Chop your own wood, and it will warm you twice.

**Henry Ford**

If you do the things you need to do when you need to do them, then someday you can do the things you want to do when you want to do them.

**Zig Ziglar**

Knowing is not enough, we must apply. Willing is not enough, we must do.

**Geothe**

Always do more than is required of you.

**George S. Patton**

Things may come to those who wait, but only things left by those who hustle.

**Abraham Lincoln**

If I had to sum up in a word what makes a good manager, It's decisiveness. You can use the fanciest computers to gather the numbers, but in the end you have to set a timetable and act.

**Lee Iacocca**

Two roads diverged in a wood, and I...I took the one less traveled by, and that has made all the difference.

**Robert Frost**

An old man was asked what had robbed him of joy in his life. His reply was, "Things that never happened."

**Dale Carnegie**

A good plan implemented today is better than a perfect plan implemented tomorrow.

**George S. Patton**

Do what you can, with what you have, where you are.

**Theodore Roosevelt**

It is always your next move.

**Napoleon Hill**

Nothing preaches better than the act.

**Benjamin Franklin**

You are what you think. You are what you go for. You are what you do.

**Bob Richards**

You can't cross the sea merely by standing and staring at the water.

**Rabindranath Tagore**

Who dares nothing, need hope for nothing.

**Johann Friedrich Von Schiller**

---

Do not go where the path may lead, go instead where there is no path and leave a trail.

**Ralph Waldo Emerson**

The invariable mark of wisdom is to see the miraculous in the common.

**Ralph Waldo Emerson**

In the universe, there are things that are known, and things that are unknown, and in between, there are doors.

**William Blake**

If we all did the things we are capable of doing, we would literally astound ourselves.

**Thomas Alva Edison**

It is only when we truly know and understand that we have a limited time on earth and that we have no way of knowing when our time is up that we will begin to live each day to the fullest, as if it were the only one we had.

**Elizabeth Kubler-Ross**

Fortune and love befriend the bold.

**Ovid**

People travel to wonder at the height of mountains, at the huge waves of the sea, at the long courses of rivers, at the vast compass of the ocean, at the circular motion of the stars; and they pass by themselves without wondering.

**St. Augustine**

When you come to a fork in the road, take it.

**Yogi Berra**

Life is either a daring adventure or nothing.

**Helen Keller**

There are two kinds of adventurers: those who go truly hoping to find adventure and those who go secretly hoping they won't.

**William Trogdon**

One comes to believe whatever one repeats to oneself sufficiently often, whether the statement be true of false. It comes to be dominating thought in one's mind.

**Robert Collier**

First say to yourself what you would be; and then do what you have to do.

**Epictetus**

Our subconscious minds have no sense of humor, play no jokes and cannot tell the difference between reality and an imagined thought or image. What we continually think about eventually will manifest in our lives.

**Sidney Madwed**

We cannot always control our thoughts, but we can control our words, and repetition impresses the subconscious, and we are then master of the situation.

**Florence Scovel Shinn**

You must begin to think of yourself as becoming the person you want to be.

**David Viscott**

It's the repetition of affirmations that leads to belief. And once that belief becomes a deep conviction, things begin to happen.

**Claude M. Bristol**

Don't be afraid to give up the good to go for the great.

**Kenny Rogers**

---

As long as you're going to think anyway, think big.

**Donald Trump**


Ambition never comes to an end.

**Yoshida Kenko**


Get action. Seize the moment. Man was never intended to become an oyster.

**Theodore Roosevelt**


I never worry about action, only inaction.

**Winston Churchill**


Our ambition should be to rule ourselves, the true kingdom for each one of us; and true progress is to know more, and be more, and to do more.

**Sr John Lubbock**


If you have a great ambition, take as big a step as possible in the direction of fulfilling it. The step may only be a tiny one, but trust that it may be the largest one possible for now.

**Mildred Mcafee**


Keep your feet on the ground and keep reaching for the stars.

**Casey Kasem**


The men who succeed are the efficient few. They are the few who have the ambition and will power to develop themselves.

**Herbert N. Casson**


Big results require big ambitions.

**James Champy**

I had ambition not only to go farther than any man had ever been before, but as far as it was possible for a man to go.

**James R. Cook**

Without ambition one starts nothing. Without work one finishes nothing. The prize will not be sent to you. You have to win it.

**Ralph Waldo Emerson**

Ambition is the germ from which all growth of nobleness proceeds.

**Thomas Dunn English**

I've got a great ambition to die of exhaustion rather than boredom.

**Angus Grossart**

Ambition is so powerful a passion in the human breast, that however high we reach we are never satisfied.

**Niccolo Machiavelli**

Appreciation can make a day, even change a life. Your willingness to put it into words is all that is necessary.

**Margaret Cousins**

There is more hunger for love and appreciation in this world than for bread.

**Mother Teresa**

Courtesies of a small and trivial character are the ones which strike deepest in the gratefully and appreciating heart.

**Henry Clay**

I would rather be able to appreciate things I can not have than to have things I am not able to appreciate.

**Elbert Hubbard**

Finish each day and be done with it. You have done what you could; some blunders and absurdities have crept in; forget them as soon as you can. Tomorrow is a new day; you shall begin it serenely and with too high a spirit to be encumbered with your old nonsense.

**Ralph Waldo Emerson**

Appreciation is a wonderful thing. It makes what is excellent in others belong to us as well.

**Voltaire**

What happens to a man is less significant than what happens within him.

**Louis L. Mann**

An inexhaustible good nature is one of the most precious gifts of heaven, spreading itself like oil over the troubled sea of thought, and keeping the mind smooth and equable in the roughest weather.

**Washington Irving**

There are no menial jobs, only menial attitudes.

**William John Bennett**

Enter every activity without giving mental recognition to the possibility of defeat. Concentrate on your strengths instead of your weaknesses, on your powers instead of your problems.

**Paul J. Meyer**

I never expect to lose. Even when I'm the underdog, I still prepare a victory speech.

**H. Jackson Brown, Jr.**

We tend to live up to our expectations.

**Earl Nightingale**

He who has a thousand friends has not a friend to spare, while he who has one enemy shall meet him everywhere.

**Ralph Waldo Emerson**

It is not the position, but the disposition.

**J. E. Dinger**

Take the attitude of a student; never be too big to ask questions, never know too much to learn something new.

**Og Mandino**

I had no ambition to make a fortune. Mere money-making has never been my goal, I had an ambition to build.

**John D. Rockefeller**

Our attitude toward life determines life's attitude towards us.

**Earl Nightingale**

Attitudes are more important than facts.

**Karl A. Menninger**

An optimist may see a light where there is none, but why must the pessimist always run to blow it out?

**Michel De Saint-Pierre**

Pretend that every single person you meet has a sign around his or her neck that says, Make Me Feel Important. Not only will you succeed in sales, you will succeed in life.

**Mary Kay Ash**

Throw your heart over the fence and the rest will follow.

**Norman Vincent Peale**

Make your life a mission - not an intermission.

**Arnold H. Glasgow**

---

Look well to this day. Yesterday is but a dream and tomorrow is only a vision. But today well lived makes every yesterday a dream of happiness and every tomorrow a vision of hope. Look well therefore to this day.

**Francis Gray**

Live as you will have wished to have lived when you are dying.

**Christian Furchtegott Gellert**

Forget about all the reasons why something may not work. You only need to find one good reason why it will.

**Dr. Robert Anthony**

I take nothing for granted. I now have only good days, or great days.

**Lance Armstrong**

High expectations are the key to everything.

**Sam Walton**

A cloudy day is no match for a sunny disposition.

**William Arthur Ward**

Believe and act as if it were impossible to fail.

**Charles Kettering**

A pessimist is one who makes difficulties of his opportunities and an optimist is one who makes opportunities of his difficulties.

**Harry Truman**

Don't bother just to be better than your contemporaries or predecessors. Try to be better than yourself.

**William Faulkner**

The time is always right to do what is right.

**Martin Luther King, Jr.**

It is not because things are difficult that we do not dare, it is because we do not dare that they are difficult.

**Seneca**

It is one of the most beautiful compensations of life, that no man can sincerely try to help another without helping himself.

**Ralph Waldo Emerson**

Success doesn't make you and failure doesn't break you.

**Zig Ziglar**

To change and to change for the better are two different things.

**German proverb**

Nothing is good or bad, but thinking makes it so.

**William Shakespeare**

My father gave me the greatest gift anyone could give another person, he believed in me.

**Jim Valvano**

# Chapter 18

My attitude is never to be satisfied, never enough, never.

**Bela Karolyi**

There is little difference in people, but that little difference makes a big difference. That little difference is attitude. The big difference is whether it is positive or negative.

**W. Clement Stone**

We cannot change our past. We can not change the fact that people act in a certain way. We can not change the inevitable. The only thing we can do is play on the one string we have, and that is our attitude.

**Charles Swindoll**

Dream as if you'll live forever ... live as if you'll die today.

**James Dean**

There are only two ways to live your life. One is as though nothing is a miracle. The other is as if everything is.

**Albert Einstein**

Never underestimate the heart of a champion.

**Rudy Tomjanovich**

I would rather make my name than inherit it.

**W.M. Thackeray**

A champion hates to lose even more than she loves to win.

**Chris Evert**

It is a shameful thing for the soul to faint while the body still perseveres.

**Marcus Aurelius Antoninus**

No man is ever whipped, until he quits - in his own mind.

**Napoleon Hill**

Weakness of attitude becomes weakness of character.

**Albert Einstein**

The only way around is through.

**Robert Frost**

The spirit, the will to win, and the will to excel are the things that endure. These qualities are so much more important than the events that occur.

**Vincent Lombardi**

I love living. I have some problems with my life, but living is the best thing they've come up with so far.

**Neil Simon**

We can let circumstances rule us, or we can take charge and rule our lives from within.

**Earl Nightingale**

Who hath not known ill fortune, never knew himself, or his own virtue.

**Mallett**

To laugh often and much; to win the respect of intelligent people and the affection of children; to earn the appreciation of honest critics and endure the betrayal of false friends; to appreciate beauty, to find the best in others; to leave the world a little better; whether by a healthy child, a garden patch or a redeemed social condition; to know even one life has breathed easier because you have lived. This is the meaning of success.

**Ralph Waldo Emerson**

We could never learn to be brave and patient, if there were only joy in the world.

**Helen Keller**

I believe that anyone can conquer fear by doing the things he fears to do.

**Helen Keller**

Fear is the main source of superstition, and one of the main sources of cruelty. To conquer fear is the beginning of wisdom.

**Bertrand Russell**

Decision is the spark that ignites action. Until a decision is made, nothing happens.... Decision is the courageous facing of issues, knowing that if they are not faced, problems will remain forever unanswered.

**Bertrand Wilbertforce**

The greatest mistake you can make in life is to be continually fearing that you will make one.

**Elbert Hubbard**

He who fears being conquered is sure of defeat.

**Napoleon**

Coward die many times before their deaths; the valiant never taste of death but once.

**William Shakespeare**

Keep your face to the sunshine and you cannot see the shadows.

**Helen Keller**

Happiness comes to those who are moving toward something they want very much to happen. And it almost always involves making someone else happy.

**Earl Nightingale**

To insure good health: Eat lightly, breathe deeply, live moderately, cultivate cheerfulness, and maintain an interest in life.

**William Londen**

Cheerfulness is a very great help in fostering the virtue of charity. Cheerfulness itself is a virtue.

**Lawrence G. Lovasik**

Inner sunshine warms not only the heart of the owner, but all who come in contact with it.

**J. T. Fields**

Cheerfulness is full of significance: it suggests good health, a clear conscience, and a soul at peace with all human nature.

**Charles Kingsley**

The best way to cheer yourself up is to try to cheer somebody else up.

**Mark Twain**

The path to cheerfulness is to sit cheerfully and to act and speak as if cheerfulness were already there.

**William James**

Cheerfulness and contentment are great beautifiers and are famous preservers of youthful looks.

**Charles Dickens**

Cheerfulness is the best promoter of health and is as friendly to the mind as to the body.

**Joseph Addison**

Look for your choices, pick the best one, then go with it.

**Pat Riley**

It is always your next move.

**Napoleon Hill**

You are the person who has to decide. Whether you'll do it or toss it aside; You are the person who makes up your mind. Whether you'll lead or will linger behind. Whether you'll try for the goal that's afar. Or just be contented to stay where you are.

**Edgar A. Guest**

Focus on where you want to go, not on what you fear.

**Anthony Robbins**

We've got to have a dream if we are going to make a dream come true.

**Denis Waitley**

Instead of looking at life as a narrowing funnel, we can see it ever widening to choose the things we want to do, to take the wisdom we've learned and create something.

**Liz Carpenter**

Man's power of choice enables him to think like an angel or a devil, a king or a slave. Whatever he chooses, mind will create and manifest.

**Frederick Bailes**

Your life is the sum result of all the choices you make, both consciously and unconsciously. If you can control the process of choosing, you can take control of all aspects of your life. You can find the freedom that comes from being in charge of yourself.

**Robert F. Bennett**

You cannot raise a man up by calling him down.

**William Boetcker**

My mother's menu consisted of two choices: Take it or leave it.

**Buddy Hackett**

Enthusiasm releases the drive to carry you over obstacles and adds significance to all you do.

**Norman Vincent Peale**

The last of the human freedoms is to choose one's attitudes.

**Victor Frank**

Destiny is not a matter of chance, it is a matter of choice; it is not a thing to be waited for, it is a thing to be achieved.

**William Jennings Bryan**

The quality, not the longevity, of one's life is what is important.

**Dr. Martin Luther King, Jr.**

The quality of a person's life is in direct proportion to their commitment excellence, regardless of their chosen field of endeavor.

**Vincent Lombardi**

Associate yourself with men of good quality if you esteem your own reputation. It is better be alone than in bad company.

**George Washington**

Quality is never an accident; it is always the result of high intention, sincere effort, intelligent direction and skillful execution; it represents the wise choice of many alternatives.

**William A. Foster**

Whatever we plant in our subconscious mind and nourish with repetition and emotion will one day become a reality.

**Earl Nightingale**

Your goals, minus your doubts, equal your reality.

**Ralph Marston**

Reality leaves a lot to the imagination.

**John Lennon**


The real man smiles in trouble, gathers strength from distress, and grows brave by reflection.

**Thomas Paine**


Always vote for principle, though you may vote alone, and you may cherish the sweetest reflection that your vote is never lost.

**John Quincy Adams**


By three methods we may learn wisdom: First, by reflection, which is noblest; Second, by imitation, which is easiest; and third by experience, which is the bitterest.

**Confucius**


Each of us is here for a brief sojourn; for what purpose he knows not, though he senses it. But without deeper reflection one knows from daily life that one exists for other people.

**Albert Einstein**


Treasure your relationships, not your possessions.

**Anthony J D'Angelo**


If you wish your merit to be known, acknowledge that of other people.

**Asian Proverb**


To handle yourself, use your head; to handle others, use your heart.

**Eleanor Roosevelt**


If I can stop one heart from breaking, I shall not live in vain; If I can ease one life from aching, or cool one pain, or help one fainting robin unto his nest again, I shall not live in vain.

**Emily Dickinson**

Respect a man, and he will do all the more.

**John Wooden**

If one doesn't respect oneself one can have neither love nor respect for others.

**Ayn Rand**

We confide in our strength, without boasting of it; we respect that of others, without fearing it.

**Thomas Jefferson**

They cannot take away our self-respect if we do not give it to them.

**Mahatma Gandhi**

We must build a new world, a far better world - one in which the eternal dignity of man is respected.

**Harry S. Truman**

I still need more healthy rest in order to work at my best. My health is the main capital I have and I want to administer it intelligently.

**Ernest Hemingway**

If you rest, you rust.

**Helen Hayes**

Rest is not idleness, and to lie sometimes on the grass on a summer day listening to the murmur of water, or watching the clouds float across the sky, is hardly a waste of time.

**Sir John Lubbock**

The time to relax is when you don't have time for it.

**Sidney J. Harris**

It's in your moments of decision that your destiny is shaped.

**Anthony Robbins**

Every now and then go away, have a little relaxation, for when you come back to your work your judgment will be surer. Go some distance away because then the work appears smaller and more of it can be taken in at a glance and a lack of harmony and proportion is more readily seen.

**Leonardo Da Vinci**

Rest is the sweet sauce of labor.

**Plutarch**

The starting point of all achievement is desire. Keep this constantly in mind. Weak desires bring weak results, just as a small amount of fire makes a small amount of heat.

**Napoleon Hill**

You always succeed in producing a result.

**Anthony Robbins**

The achievements of an organization are the results of the combined effort of each individual.

**Vincent Lombardi**

Every choice you make has an end result.

**Zig Ziglar**

Those who trust to chance must abide by the results of chance.

**Calvin Coolidge**

If you want to be successful, find someone who has achieved the results you want and copy what they do and you'll achieve the same results.

**Anthony Robbins**

Our lives improve only when we take chances - and the first and most difficult risk we can take is to be honest with ourselves.

**Walter Anderson**

Take a chance! All life is a chance. The man who goes the furthest is generally the one who is willing to do and dare. The 'sure thing' boat never gets far from shore.

**Dale Carnegie**

And the trouble is, if you don't risk anything, you risk even more.

**Erica Jong**

Entrepreneurs are risk takers, willing to roll the dice with their money or reputation on the line in support of an idea or enterprise. They willingly assume responsibility for the success or failure of a venture and are answerable for all its facets. The buck not only stops at their desks, it starts there too.

**Victor Kiam**

Look at everything as though you were seeing it for the first time or last time. Then your time on earth will be filled with glory.

**Betty Smith**

It is the familiar that usually eludes us in life. What is before our nose is what we see last.

**William Barrett**

Discovery consists of looking at the same thing as everyone else and thinking something different.

**Albert Szent-Gyorgyi**

Vision: the art of seeing the invisible.

**Jonathan Swift**

The question is not what you look at, but what you see.

**Henry David Thoreau**

The obscure we see eventually. The completely obvious, it seems, takes longer.

**Edward R. Murrow**

The greatest thing a human soul ever does in this world is to see something, and tell what it saw in a plain way. Hundreds of people can talk for one who can think, but thousands can think for one who can see. To see clearly is poetry, prophecy, and religion - all in one.

**John Ruskin**

What we see depends mainly on what we look for.

**John Lubbock**

Confidence, like art, never comes from having all the answers; it comes from being open to all the questions.

**Earl Gray Stevens**

If you have no confidence in self, you are twice defeated in the race of life. With confidence, you have won even before you have started.

**Marcus Garvey**

Somehow I can't believe that there are any heights that can't be scaled by a man who knows the secrets of making dreams come true. This special secret, it seems to me, can be summarized in four C s. They are curiosity, confidence, courage, and constancy, and the greatest of all is confidence. When you believe in a thing, believe in it all the way, implicitly and unquestionable.

**Walt Disney**

You grow up the day you have your first real laugh - at yourself.

**Ethel Barrymore**

Give me where to stand, and I will move the earth.

**Archimedes**

---

One man who has a mind and knows it can always beat ten men who haven't and don't.

**George Bernard Shaw**

Having once decided to achieve a certain task, achieve it at all costs of tedium and distaste. The gain in self-confidence of having accomplished a tiresome labor is immense.

**Thomas A. Bennett**

One of the greatest moments in anybody's developing experience is when he no longer tries to hide from himself but determines to get acquainted with himself as he really is.

**Norman Vincent Peale**

The good Lord gave you a body that can stand most anything. It's your mind you have to convince.

**Vincent Lombardi**

If it is to be, it is up to me.

**William Johnson**

You are educated when you have the ability to listen to almost anything without losing your temper or self-confidence.

**Robert Frost**

Confidence is a very fragile thing.

**Joe Montana**

Do not attempt to do a thing unless you are sure of yourself; but do not relinquish it simply because someone else is not sure of you.

**Stewart E. White**

Part of being a champ is acting like a champ. You have to learn how to win and not run away when you lose. Everyone has bad stretches and real successes. Either way, you have to be careful not to lose your confidence or get too confident.

**Nancy Kerrigan**

You've got to take the initiative and play your game. In a decisive set, confidence is the difference.

**Chris Evert**

Confidence...thrives on honesty, on honor, on the sacredness of obligations, on faithful protection and on unselfish performance. Without them it cannot live.

**Franklin D. Roosevelt**

One important key to success is self confidence. An important key to self confidence is preparation.

**Arthur Ashe**

Confidence is contagious and so is lack of confidence, and a customer will recognize both.

**Vincent Lombardi**

Talent is only the starting point.

**Irving Berlin**

Look well into thyself; there is a source of strength which will always spring up if thou wilt always look there.

**Marcus Antoninus**

It is for us to pray not for tasks equal to our powers, but for powers equal to our tasks, to go forward with a great desire forever beating at the door of our hearts as we travel toward our distant goal.

**Helen Keller**

Strength does not come from physical capacity. It comes from an indomitable will.

**Mahatma Gandhi**

Good actions give strength to ourselves and inspire good actions in others.

**Plato**

Nothing is so strong as gentleness. Nothing is so gentle as real strength.

**Frances de Sales**

The talent of success is nothing more than doing what you can do well and doing well whatever you do.

**Henry Wadsworth Longfellow**

The elevator to success is out of order. You'll have to use the stairs ... one step at a time.

**Joe Girard**

To laugh often and much; to win the respect of intelligent people and the affection of children; to earn the appreciation of honest critics and endure the betrayal of false friends; to appreciate beauty; to find the best in others; to leave the world a bit better, whether by a healthy child, a garden patch or a redeemed social condition; to know even one life has breathed easier because you have lived. This is to have succeeded.

**Ralph Waldo Emerson**

How to succeed? Try hard enough.

**Malcolm Forbes**

You only have to do a very few things right in your life so long as you don't do too many things wrong.

**Warren Buffett**

Success is dependent upon the glands – sweat glands.

**Zig Ziglar**

The successful man will profit from his mistakes and try again in a different way.

**Dale Carnegie**

Six essential qualities are the key to success: sincerity, personal integrity, humility, courtesy, wisdom, charity.

**William Menninger**

Success and rest don't sleep together.

**Russian proverb**

The secret of success is to know something nobody else knows.

**Aristotle Onassis**

Real success comes in small portions day by day. You need to take pleasure in life's daily little treasures. It is the most important thing in measuring success.

**Denis Waitley**

For everyone of us that succeeds, it's because there's somebody there to show you the way out. The light doesn't always necessarily have to be in your family; for me it was teachers and school.

**Oprah Winfrey**

I never knew an early-rising, hard-working, prudent man, careful of his earnings, and strictly honest who complained of bad luck.

**Henry Ward Beecher**

If you work just for money, you'll never make it. But if you love what you are doing, and always put the customer first, success will be yours.

**Ray Kroc**

Success without honor is an unseasoned dish; it will satisfy your hunger, but it won't taste good.

**Joe Paterno**

Success is not the key to happiness. Happiness is the key to success. If you love what you are doing, you will be successful.

**Albert Schweitzer**

Success is how high you bounce when you hit bottom.

**George S. Patton**

Success is going from failure to failure without losing your enthusiasm.

**Abraham Lincoln**

When building a team, I always search first for people who love to win. If I can't find any of those, I look for people who hate to lose.

**H. Ross Perot**

Appreciate everything your associates do for the business. Nothing else can quite substitute for a few well-chosen, well-timed, sincere words of praise. They're absolutely free and worth a fortune.

**Sam Walton**

Behind every able man, there are always other able men.

**Chinese Proverb**

Individual commitment to a group effort - that is what makes a team work, a company work, a society work, a civilization work.

**Vincent Lombardi**

A boss creates fear, a leader confidence. A boss fixes blame, a leader corrects mistakes. A boss knows all, a leader asks questions. A boss makes work drudgery, a leader makes it interesting. A boss is interested in himself or herself, a leader is interested in the group.

**Russell H. Ewing**

---

There's nothing greater in the world than when somebody on the team does something good, and everybody gathers around to pat him on the back.

**Billy Martin**

I would rather fail in a cause that will ultimately triumph than to triumph in a cause that will ultimately fail.

**Woodrow Wilson**

Although there may be tragedy in your life, there's always a possibility to triumph. It doesn't matter who you are, where you come from. The ability to triumph begins with you. Always.

**Oprah Winfrey**

The harder the conflict, the more glorious the triumph. What we obtain too cheaply, we esteem too lightly; 'Tis dearness only that gives everything its value.

**Thomas Paine**

Far better is it to dare mighty things, to win glorious triumphs, even though checkered by failure than to rank with those poor spirits who neither enjoy much nor suffer much, because they live in a gray twilight that knows not victory nor defeat.

**Theodore Roosevelt**

To win without risk is to triumph without glory.

**Pierre Corneille**

History has demonstrated that the most notable winners usually encountered heartbreaking obstacles before they triumphed. They won because they refused to become discouraged by their defeats.

**B. C. Forbes**

The human spirit needs to accomplish, to achieve, to triumph to be happy.

**Ben Stein**

The only thing necessary for the triumph of evil is for good men to do nothing.

**Edmund Burke**

The potential of the average person is like a huge ocean unsailed, a new continent unexplored, a world of possibilities waiting to be released and channeled toward some great good.

**Brian Tracy**

We are not in a position in which we have nothing to work with. We already have capacities, talents, direction, missions, callings.

**Abraham H. Maslow**

Everyone has inside of him a piece of good news. The good news is that you don't know how great you can be! How much you can love! What you can accomplish! And what your potential is!

**Anne Frank**

There is no man living who isn't capable of doing more than he thinks he can do.

**Henry Ford**

In the depth of winter I finally learned that within me there lay an invincible summer.

**Albert Camus**

When a man has put a limit on what he will do, he has put a limit on what he can do.

**Charles M. Schwab**

If I were to wish for anything, I should not wish for wealth and power, but for the passionate sense of the potential, for the eye which, ever young and ardent, sees the possible. Pleasure disappoints possibility never.

**Soren Kierkegaard**

Happiness is not pleasure, it is victory.

**Zig Ziglar**

Part of the happiness of life consists not in fighting battles, but in avoiding them. A masterly retreat is in itself a victory.

**Norman Vincent Peale**

The ultimate victory in competition is derived from the inner satisfaction of knowing that you have done your best and that you have gotten the most out of what you had to give.

**Howard Cosell**

I count him braver who overcomes his desires than him who conquers his enemies; for the hardest victory is over self.

**Aristotle**

I have about concluded that wealth is a state of mind, and that anyone can acquire a wealthy state of mind by thinking rich thoughts.

**Andrew Young**

Ordinary riches can be stolen, real riches cannot. In your soul are infinitely precious things that cannot be taken from you.

**Oscar Wilde**

Wealth is the ability to fully experience life.

**Henry David Thoreau**

That some should be rich, shows that others may become rich, and, hence, is just encouragement to industry and enterprise.

**Abraham Lincoln**

He does not posses wealth that allows it to possess him.

**Benjamin Franklin**

If we command our wealth, we shall be rich and free. If our wealth commands us, we are poor indeed.

**Edmund Burke**

The fortune which nobody sees makes a person happy and unenvied.

**Francis Bacon**

Wealth after all is a relative thing since he that has little and wants less is richer than he that has much and wants more.

**Charles Caleb Colton**

The first wealth is health.

**Ralph Waldo Emerson**

People do not lack strength; they lack will.

**Victor Hugo**

Let me win, but if I cannot win, let me be brave in the attempt.

**Special Olympics Motto**

The man who can drive himself further once the effort gets painful is the man who will win.

**Roger Bannister**

To accomplish great things, we must not only act, but also dream; not only plan, but also believe.

**Anatole France**

The reason why worry kills more people than work is that more people worry than work.

**Robert Frost**

The man who is always worrying whether or not his soul would be damned generally has a soul that isn't worth a damn.

**Oliver Wendell Holmes**

Don't worry about the world coming to an end today. It's already tomorrow in Australia.

**Charles M. Schultz**

Either write something worth reading or do something worth writing.

**Ben Franklin**

Write while the heat is in you. The writer who postpones the recording of his thoughts uses an iron which has cooled to burn a hole with. He cannot inflame the minds of his audience.

**Henry David Thoreau**

So, then, to every man his chance -- to every man, regardless of his birth, his shining golden opportunity -- to every man his right to live, to work, to be himself, to become whatever his manhood and his vision can combine to make him -- this, seeker, is the promise of America.

**Thomas Wolfe**

In the final choice a soldier's pack is not so heavy as a prisoner's chains.
**Dwight D. Eisenhower (1890-1969)**
**Military Commander and 34th US President**

Posterity! You will never know how much it cost the present generation to preserve your freedom! I hope you will make good use of it!
**- letter to Abigail Adams, April 26, 1777 John Adams (1735-1826)**
**Second U.S. President**

The most important thing a father can do for his children is to love their mother.

**Theodore Hesburgh (1917-) American, Former President of Notre Dame University**

The direst foe of courage is the fear itself, not the object of it, and the man who can overcome his own terror is a hero and more.

**George Macdonald (1824-1905) Scottish Novelist and Clergyman**

The measure of a man is what happens when nothing works and you got the guts to go on.

**Randall 'Tex' Cobb (1954-) American Boxer and Actor**

It is better by noble boldness to run the risk of being subject to half the evils we anticipate than to remain in cowardly listlessness for fear of what might happen.

**Herodotus (485 - 425BC) Greek Historian**

Physical courage, which despises all danger, will make a man brave in one way; and moral courage, which despises all opinion, will make a man brave in another.

**Charles Caleb Colton (1780-1832) English Author and Clergyman**

It is better to die on your feet than to live on your knees.

**Emiliano Zapata (1879-1919) Mexican Revolutionary**

There is no such thing as a great talent without great will-power.

**Honore De Balzac (1799-1850) French Novelist**

I think I'd like to be remembered as someone who beat the odds through just plain determination. ... that I persevered. Because I think that being somewhat of a pest to life, constantly plaguing and pursuing, will bring results.

**Sylvester Stallone (1946-) American Actor**

There is great power in a resolution that has no reservations in it -- a strong, persistent, tenacious purpose -- which burns all bridges behind it and which clears all obstacles from its path and arrives at its goal, no matter how long it may take, no matter what the sacrifice or the cost.

**Orison Swett Marsden (1850-1924) American Editor and Speaker**

Any person capable of angering you becomes your master; he can anger you only when you permit yourself to be disturbed by him.

**Epictetus (55-135 AD) Roman Philosopher**

I will permit no man to narrow and degrade my soul by making me hate him.

**Booker T. Washington (1856-1915)**
**American Educator and Black Leader**

Make yourself an honest man, and then you may be sure that there is one less scoundrel in the world.

**Thomas Carlyle (1795-1881) Scottish Writer**

The shortest and surest way to live with honor in the world is to be in reality what we would appear to be.

**Socrates (469-399 BC) Greek Philosopher**

I hope I shall always possess firmness and virtue enough to maintain what I consider the most enviable of all titles, the character of the "Honest Man."

**George Washington**

The naked truth is always better than the best dressed lie.

**Ann Landers, born 1918**

There is a sense of exhilaration that comes from facing head-on the hard truths and saying, "We will never give up. We will never capitulate. It might take a long time, but we will find a way to prevail."

**Jim Collins, from his book, Good to Great**

Life is an opportunity, benefit from it. Life is a beauty, admire it. Life is a dream, realize it. Life is a challenge, meet it. Life is a duty, complete it. Life is a game, play it. Life is a promise, fulfill it. Life is sorrow, overcome it. Life is a song, sing it. Life is a struggle, accept it. Life is a tragedy, confront it. Life is an adventure, dare it. Life is luck, make it. Life is life, fight for it!

**Mother Teresa (1910-1997)**

I think the purpose of life is to be useful, to be responsible, to be honorable, to be compassionate. It is, after all, to matter: to count, to stand for something, to have made some difference that you lived at all.

**Leo C. Rosten (1908-1977) American Writer**

Live as you will wish to have lived when you are dying.

**Christian Furchtegott Gellert (1715-1769)**
**German Poet and Moralist**

Fear less, hope more; whine less, breathe more; talk less, say more; love more, and all good things will be yours.

**Swedish proverb**

The various religions are like different roads converging on the same point. What difference does it make if we follow different routes, provided we arrive at the same destination.

**Mohandas Karamchand Gandhi (1869-1948) Indian Nationalist**

As long as the day lasts, let's give it all we've got.

**David O. McKay (1873-1970) American Religious Leader**

There was no such thing as half-trying. Whether it was running a race or catching a football, competing in school -- we were to try. And we were to try harder than anyone else. We might not be the best, and none of us were, but we were to make the effort to be the best.

**Senator Robert F. Ken**
**nedy, in a tribute to his father, Joseph P. Kennedy**

---

The person who says it cannot be done should not interrupt the person doing it.

**Chinese proverb**

When nothing is sure, everything is possible.

**Margaret Drabble (1939-) English Novelist**

This life we have is short, so let us leave a mark for people to remember - explaining why he adopted and educated 69 orphan children.

**Kip Keino (1940-) Kenyan Olympic Gold Medallist in Track**

Man's greatest actions are performed in minor struggles. Life, misfortune, isolation, abandonment and poverty are battlefields which have their heroes - obscure heroes who are at times greater than illustrious heroes.

**Victor Hugo (1802-1885) French Writer**

Life's about friendships, the way you love your partner, the way you care for your children. That is what life is about. Not anything about earning a hundred zillion dollars because you toured America more than anyone else. I want life to be about creativity.

**Joe Strummer, former lead singer for the Clash rock band.**

To fulfill a dream, to be allowed to sweat over lonely labor, to be given a chance to create, is the meat and potatoes of life. The money is the gravy.

**Bette Davis (1908-1989) American Actress**

It is wonderful to be in on the creation of something, see it used, and then walk away and smile at it.

**Lady Bird Johnson (1912- ) American First Lady**

What I must do is all that concerns me, not what the people think.

**Ralph Waldo Emerson (1803-1882) American Poet and Essayist**

In dealings between men, truth, sincerity and integrity are of the utmost importance to the felicity of life.

**Benjamin Franklin**

Yours is not the less noble because no drum beats before you when you go out into your daily battlefields, and no crowds shout about your coming when you return from your daily victory or defeat.

**Robert Louis Stevenson (1850-1894) Scottish Novelist**

There is nothing noble in being superior to some other man. The true nobility is in being superior to your previous self.

**Hindu proverb**

The nobler sort of man emphasizes the good qualities in others, and does not accentuate the bad. The inferior does the reverse.

**Confucius (551-479 BC) Chinese Philosopher**

There is only one real failure in life that is possible, and that is, not to be true to the best one knows.

**John Farrar (1945-) Australian Composer**

Respect for the fragility and importance of an individual life is still the mark of an educated man.

**Norman Cousins (1915-1990) American Author and Humanitarian**

Determine that a thing can and shall be done, and then we shall find the way.

**Abraham Lincoln (1809-1865)**

## Chapter 19
# MY FAVORITE QUOTES

*The only thing necessary for the triumph of evil is for good men to do nothing.*

**Edmund Burke**

*If I had six hours to chop down a tree, I'd spend the first hour sharpening the ax.*

**Abraham Lincoln**

*Holding on to anger is like grasping a hot coal with the intent of throwing it at someone else; you are the one getting burned.*

**Buddha**

*Never, never, never, never give up.*

**Winston Churchill**

*Yesterday ended last night. Every day is a new beginning. Learn the skill of forgetting. And move on.*

**Norman Vincent Peale**

*How do you go from where you are to where you want to be? I think you have to have an enthusiasm for life. You have to have a dream, a goal and you have to be willing to work for it.*

**Jim Valvano**

*You've got to get to the stage in life where going for it is more important than winning or losing.*

**Arthur Ashe**

*For every minute you are angry you lose sixty seconds of happiness.*

**Ralph Waldo Emerson**

"HAPPINESS"

*The best way to cheer yourself up is to try to cheer somebody else up.*
**Mark Twain**

*Once you learn to quit, it becomes a habit.*
**Vincent Lombardi**

*Do not despise the bottom rungs in the ascent to greatness.*
**Publilius Syrus**

*The indispensable first step to getting the things you want out of life is this: decide what you want.*
**Ben Stein**

*Energy and persistence alter all things.*
**Benjamin Franklin**

*It takes as much energy to wish as it does to plan.*
**Eleanor Roosevelt**

*If people around you aren't going anywhere, if their dreams are no bigger than hanging out on the corner, or if they're dragging you down, get rid of them. Negative people can sap your energy so fast, and they can take your dreams from you, too.*
**Earvin "Magic" Johnson**

*Flatter me, and I may not believe you. Criticize me, and I may not like you. Ignore me, and I may not forgive you. Encourage me, and I may not forget you.*
**William Arthur**

*Words are, of course, the most powerful drug used by mankind*
**Rudyard Kipling**

*Work like you don't need the money. Love like you've never been hurt. Dance like nobody is watching.*

**Mark Twain / Samuel Clements**

*Ability may get you to the top, but it takes character to keep you there.*

**John Wooden**

*I have not failed. I've just found 10,000 ways that won't work.*

**Thomas Edison**

*He who has health, has hope. And he who has hope, has everything.*

**Arabian Proverb**

*Everyone who got where he is had to begin where he was.*

**Richard L. Evans**

*It's how you deal with failure that determines how you achieve success.*

**David Feherty**

*The time is always right to do what is right.*

**Martin Luther King**

*If you want happiness for an hour, take a nap. If you want happiness for a day, go fishing. If you want happiness for a year, inherit a fortune. If you want happiness for a lifetime, help somebody.*

**Chinese Proverb**

*If we study the lives of great men and women carefully and unemotionally we find that, invariably, greatness was developed, tested and revealed through the darker periods of their lives. One of the largest tributaries of the RIVER OF GREATNESS is always the STREAM OF ADVERSITY.*

**Cavett Robert**

*You have to stay in shape. My grandmother, she started walking five miles a day when she was 60. She's 97 today and we don't know where the hell she is.*

**Ellen Degeneres**

*Good timber does not grow with ease. The stonger the wind the stronger the trees.*

**Williard Marriott**

*It doesn't take talent to hustle.*

**H. Jackson Brown**

*An army of sheep led by a lion would defeat an army of lions led by a sheep.*

**Arab proverb**

*Fall seven times; stand up eight.*

**Japanese Proverb**

*You ask what our aim is. I can answer in one word - VICTORY. Victory at all costs, Victory in spite of fear, Victory, however long and hard the road may be.*

**Winston Churchill**

*As long as you're going to think anyway, think big.*

**Donald Trump**

*There are no menial jobs, only menial attitudes.*

**William John Bennett**

*Although there may be tragedy in your life, there's always a possibility to triumph. It doesn't matter who you are, where you come from. The ability to triumph begins with you. Always.*

**Oprah Winfrey**

*The person who says it cannot be done should not interrupt the person doing it.*

**Chinese proverb**

---

*There is nothing noble in being superior to some other man. The true nobility is in being superior to your previous self.*

**Hindu proverb**

*Failure is nature's plan to prepare you for great responsibilities.*

**Napoleon Hill**

The Author: Ian Howard

9 780998 578187